AMERICAN FASHION

© 2007 Assouline Publishing
601 West 26th Street, 18th floor
New York, NY 10001, USA
Tel.: 212 989-6810   Fax: 212 647-0005
www.assouline.com

Color separation by Luc Alexis Chasleries
Printed in China

ISBN: 978 275940 1611

AMERICAN FASHION

COUNCIL OF FASHION DESIGNERS OF AMERICA

Charlie Scheips

For Lori
Ever best
Charlie S

ASSOULINE

CONTENTS

LETTER FROM THE PRESIDENT

Diane von Furstenberg   7

THE MAKING OF AMERICAN FASHION   9

FASHION IN CONTEXT   18

1929/1938   Dramatic Beginnings   34

1939/1946   Wartime Invention and Expansion   64

1947/1960   Back to the Future   96

1961/1971   Space Age Youthquake   138

1972/1980   American Fashion Arrives   168

1981/1999   Brand Name Stars   206

2000...   Contemporary Directions   252

AMERICAN DESIGNERS   298

CFDA AWARD WINNERS   313

INDEX AND CREDITS   316

ACKNOWLEDGMENTS   320

LETTER FROM THE PRESIDENT

Diane von Furstenberg

The American Dream…this evocative feeling of making it happen in America is very symbolic of the history of fashion in America. Thousands of immigrants, penniless and hopeful for a better life, came to this country as seamstresses, tailors, printers, and designers, weaving together a fabric that is today *American Fashion*…an extraordinary and colorful history of eight decades of the American fashion industry…

In 1962, the CFDA was founded to promote and protect fashion designers working in the United States. Today, the CFDA has become the country's premiere fashion advocacy group, supporting a powerful network of over 275 emerging designers, as well as the marquee names known throughout the world. It is a very unique organization that marries giving with receiving to create a continuous cycle of support and important partnerships that celebrate American fashion every day.

As a designer and current President of the CFDA, I would like to acknowledge the outstanding leadership the CFDA has experienced to date. We would not be the organization we are today without the imagination and innovation of our past presidents. We thank Sydney Wragge, Norman Norell, Oscar de la Renta, Herbert Kasper, Bill Blass, Mary McFadden, Perry Ellis, Carolyn Roehm, and Stan Herman for selflessly dedicating themselves to the CFDA throughout the years, while simultaneously balancing their own design enterprises.

Finally, I would like to thank Assouline for partnering with the CFDA on this project, writer Charlie Scheips, and all of the writers, photographers, and artists involved who allowed us to use their work. I would also like to thank Steven Kolb, Lisa Smilor, and their team for their passion for and dedication to the CFDA, and for their time and effort in making *American Fashion* come to life. Finally, my heartfelt gratitude goes out to the hundreds of designers who donated time and precious personal archives to make this celebratory volume possible. They are the stars of this book, and together we at the CFDA salute them all for sharing their lives with us through …

Diane Van Furstenberg

CFDA, 1990
Opposite CFDA members rallied in New York City's Garment District to launch Seventh on Sale, a three-day shopping extravaganza organized with *Vogue* that raised $4.7 million for HIV/AIDS services.

Mainbocher, ca. 1939
Previous page, left Mainbocher's triumph in black net with long tight sleeves and pleated skirt. Shot by Man Ray.

THE MAKING OF AMERICAN FASHION

Charlie Scheips

John Singer Sargent, 1884
Above Amercian-born Madame Pierre Gautreau poses for Sargent's famous painting *Madame X.*

Luis Estévez, 1960
Opposite Dina Merrill, in a gown by Luis Estévez, poses for fashion photographer Milton H. Greene for *Life* magazine.

American Fashion is a celebration of the past eight decades of modern and contemporary American fashion. It is a visual journey spanning from its early protean creators in Hollywood and New York during the 1930s to their contemporary progeny—the internationally known American stars of world fashion. The history of American fashion, of course, precedes this book's focus dating back to the founding of the country. Most significantly, the entire scope of fashion in America represents a trajectory of progress, interpollination, and invention—like America herself. It's a long and meandering history, and at times irreparably altered by major political and economic upheaval. But, ultimately, America's fashion industry has always been able to adapt and move forward. As fashion in America evolved, it remained long overshadowed by Europe—just as European art took precedence over American art, architecture, and design until the onset of World War II. And while these old-world influences continue, even today, to compete with and sometimes inspire our native productions, we are no longer a derivative offshoot but instead a global partner in the international world of fashion—on equal footing, and ourselves influencing Paris, Milan, London, and Tokyo. This book tells the story of how that came to be.

American fashion is pluralistic and inventive but also energetic and expansive. It is fitting with the country's founding principles that the fashion industry's progenitors come from every corner of the world. Like America's citizenry, American fashion has always seemed to have an almost prodigal ability to absorb its disparate creative sources and expressions into a collective whole. That is certainly what the founders of the Council of Fashion Designers of America (CFDA) imagined in 1962, when they joined forces in common purpose to promote and celebrate the creativity of American fashion design. Today, its outer influences have expanded to include artistic samplings and inspirations from cultures all around the globe—and, for that matter, the cosmos.

To fully comprehend American fashion's achievements in the face of the cultural, political, and economic obstacles it has faced during its history, it is worth examining its trajectory. Three distinct fashion images, spanning more than a century show how American fashion has evolved from an industry with one eye aimed toward Europe into a global player. John Singer Sargent's 1883 painting of *Madame X* is one of the great icons of American painting. The model for Sargent's painting was Madame Pierre Gautreau, the American-born wife of a wealthy French banker. For the painting, Gautreau wore a revealing couture gown of black satin in the latest style by French couturier Felix Poissineau. The celebrated beauty, with henna-colored hair, white powdered skin, and slightly rouged ears, well-known in fashionable circles of the social swirl of the belle époque, stands regally at ease and aloof with seductive allure. Gautreau epitomized *mondaine* glamour befitting a character straight from the novels of those two famed American expatriates Henry James and Edith Wharton. Originally, her jeweled strap was painted casually off shoulder—which, as it turns out, must have been the final indignity for conservative *beau monde* viewers of the Salon that year. So great was the uproar that met the painting's debut that Sargent repainted the strap firmly on Gautreau's shoulder and even went so far as to relocate to London—with the painting in tow. Gautreau herself pleaded for the painting to be removed and subsequently retired from public life.

Since then, Madame X has been the model for countless *homage* ranging from pastiche to tribute. Milton Greene's classic shot features the American actress and Post Cereal heiress Dina Merrill regally attired in Cuban-born, American fashion designer Luis Estévez's low-cut black crepe tribute to the famous Sargent painting. Originally published in *Life* magazine in 1960, the scandal that shook fashionable Paris eight decades before had evaporated to near historic oblivion. Readers of *Life* would, instead, have seen this photograph as a paean to American art history and native glamour. Merrill as Madame X is a decidedly mid-twentieth-century character. In Merrill we see a red-blooded, buxom blonde—a thoroughly American goddess seen through the scrim of the country's artistic heritage. Forty years later photographer Steven Meisel photographed Australian-born actress Nicole Kidman as Madame X, wearing a gown by Oscar de la Renta, for a 1999 issue of *Vogue*. Over 100 years separate the world of Sargent's Eurocentric belle epoque seductress, Greene's mid-century American beauty, and Meisel's contemporary international movie star. Yet together, in one pose captured and recaptured, they underscore the dramatic transformation that American fashion has undergone—from consumers of European culture to mid-century producers of American glamour, and finally to the truly global force in international fashion that America has become.

But how do we attempt to define American fashion if not by paradox and metaphor? When we speak of American art, or music, or cuisine, "American" is not a particularly instructive term in the wired, interconnected, and globally traversed-world in which we live today. Oscar de la Renta, born in the Caribbean, and trained in Spain and France in his youth, has been an American designer for more than four decades. Like American artists, composers, and chefs, their training and influences may or may not have roots in European culture and tradition. An artist may use Islamic patterns as sources, a composer may consult the *I Ching* as a compositional method for his music, or a chef may blend French haute cuisine with Asian culinary

Eleanor Lambert, ca. 1934

10

traditions to form a hybrid repast. But these artistic endeavors are better understood as unique to each artist himself. It is a painting by Philip Taaffe; a composition by John Cage; a menu by Joel Robuchon; and a dress by Oscar de la Renta, Diane von Furstenberg, or Carolina Herrera. Is it American? Does anyone really care about such borders in the current millennium? I guess we can all agree that to some degree, if any art form was made in America it is American—regardless of its content, and no matter from whence its sources or creators came. The American composer and critic Virgil Thomson perhaps made the most sense when asked what makes American music "American." He deadpanned:

"The way to write American music is simple. All you have to do is be an American and then write any kind of music you wish."

Of course, this is not to suggest that the history of American fashion has no debt to innovations by the leading couturiers of Paris. Just think of how Hudson River painters (our first native contemporary artists) took inspiration from the Barbizon school during the mid-nineteenth century. Or what of the American cubists who emulated the developments forged by Pablo Picasso and Georges Braque in the first decades of the twentieth century. Picasso himself said, "If there is something to steal, I steal it."

The rise of New York as the country's premier fashion center in the early nineteenth century marked the dawn of fashion in America as an industry. With the completion of the Erie Canal in 1825, New York soon overtook Boston and Philadelphia as the chief port for the expanding nation. An ever increasing universe of foreign and domestic importers, suppliers, and merchants soon flooded into Manhattan to take advantage of its central markets and well-connected transit routes for the exchange of goods. Although he didn't invent the sewing machine, Isaac Singer's patent for home-use machines revolutionized the industry—having lasting effects well into the middle of the twentieth century. With the enormous expansion of American power and wealth as the nineteenth century came to a close, Americans had an insatiable taste for European art, architecture, cuisine, and design. Upper-class Americans could afford the antiques, couture, and art of Europe, while the middle class was supplied with affordable facsimile reproductions that industrial mechanization and advances in transportation and distribution made possible. This appetite for all things European also instilled an increasing sense of American inferiority about European culture. Assumptions of European preeminence frequently tinged the American psyche and shaped tastes among fashionable circles in America well into the 1970s—and even remain in some circles today.

It was also at the end of the nineteenth century, however, that we saw the emergence of the first distinct and original expression of American fashion and style—the Gibson Girl, imagined by artist Charles Dana Gibson. The Gibson Girl inspired a look that would be the prevailing American fashion until the eve of World War I. Sportive and healthy, she evolved as American women began to increase their role in mainstream culture. Her archetypal uniform was an ensemble composed of a shirtwaist blouse, jacket, and long

Condé Nast, 1939
Top

William Randolph Hearst, 1908
Bottom

slim skirt—a far cry from the artificial and formal fashion espoused by Paris couturiers of the day. These ready-to-wear clothes were machine manufactured and sold as separates at varying price points at the enormous department stores such as A.T. Stewarts (founded in 1823), Lord & Taylor (founded in 1826), as well as the burgeoning upscale retailers and suppliers that congregated around Manhattan's Ladies Mile district—spanning from 14th Street and 23rd Street and between Broadway and Sixth Avenue. Men could purchase custom made and manufactured clothing offered by establishments such as Brooks Brothers (founded in 1818), who were to supply uniforms to Union soldiers during the Civil War. Handmade clothes, based on Parisian designs using both imported and domestic fabrics, complimented the wardrobes of the truly privileged American buyers of couture ensembles. These were purchased and fitted in France or at the various New York specialty shops that imported them for New York clients and were also offered at department stores across the country.

While Paris-based periodicals such as the *Gazette de Bon Temps* were sources of the latest Paris fashions for the privileged set of Caroline Astor's ballroom, it was the rise of American fashion magazines such as *Godey's Lady's Book* in 1830, *Harper's Bazaar* in 1867, *Ladies Home Journal* in 1883 and *Vogue* in 1892 that contributed most to the rising taste for, and knowledge of, the latest fashions available on both sides of the Atlantic. For much of the nineteenth century these publications popularized fashion and illustrated changing tastes and trends that could be copied by local seamstresses and tailors in cities across America. The evolution of paper dress patterns, coupled with increasingly affordable home sewing machines allowed American women to make their own clothes, or have them made locally, in current and fashionable styles. By the end of the nineteenth century, magazines and other periodicals were big business. Emerging from that business was a young advertising man who would become one of the most important figures in the history of American fashion. Saint Louis-born lawyer Condé Nast first made a name for himself during the 1890s when he brought his novel ideas of modern advertising into play at *Collier's* magazine. Using profits earned at *Collier's* he managed to buy the Ladies Home Pattern Company (later Vogue Patterns) and made his first fortune from a profitable joint venture offering sewing patterns for sale in *Ladies' Home Journal*. In 1909, after several years of negotiations, Nast used those profits to buy the unprofitable but highly influential New York society magazine *Vogue*. Unbeknownst to Nast at the time, he was also acquiring the energies of a young Edna Woolman Chase who began working for *Vogue* in 1895 and continued on after Nast purchased the magazine to become *Vogue's* editor-in-chief for an astounding 38 years—from 1914 to 1952.

Nast was attracted to the small but wealthy group of subscribers of the society weekly, often noting that he never set out to change *Vogue*—only to hire better artists and writers. He called them "class publications," and his goal for the magazine was not to have the largest subscriber base, which was *de rigueur* for the time, but instead the highest-income-bracket subscribers. Nast introduced photography as a major component of his expanding

Alexander Liberman *(far left)*, and Edna Woolman Chase *(third from right)*, 1947

magazine empire—which by 1914 included *Vanity Fair* and *House & Garden*. In 1915, he hired the internationally known society photographer Baron de Meyer, whose romantic and ethereal images of Paris fashions would dominate the look of fashion photography during the years surrounding World War I. Nast also launched the first international editions of a fashion magazine: British *Vogue* in 1916 and French *Vogue* in 1920. His competitors soon followed suit. International editions of magazines are so influential today, that it is surprising that few are aware of their completely American origin. During the 1990s, European magazine publishers would reverse the trend with American editions of magazines such as *Elle*.

For Nast's generation, born on the eve of the twentieth century, the lifestyle changes ushered in by development of the automobile, phonograph, radio, motion pictures, and airplanes were extraordinary. Women increasingly played a larger part in American society; drawn together by the suffrage movement, they achieved the right to vote in 1920. The appearance of women's colleges throughout the country coupled with more and more opportunities in the workplace also caused major societal changes. Charitable work for organizations such as the Junior League and the vital volunteerism of American women during World War I in organizations like the Red Cross, were equally transformative. During World War I, in both America and Europe, fashionable American women such as decorator Elsie de Wolfe (later Lady Mendl), heiress Ann Morgan, and theater producer Bessie Marbury enlistied society and expatriate artists from Gertrude Stein to Edith Wharton to assist in the war effort. When fears of New York being cut off from Paris fashion arose, *Vogue's* Edna Chase mounted a charity fashion show featuring New York–based designs from the prominent department stores and manufacturers of the era. But during the 1920s, Paris styles still dominated and influenced American manufacturing, as French designers became increasingly known by name. For the most part, American department store buyers went seasonally to Paris to view the collections and either brought back sketches or the garments themselves to reproduce in the United States.

Fashion ilustration dominated the way in which American women learned of the latest styles. When the already legendary photographer Edward Steichen was named chief photographer for *Vogue* in 1923, the die was cast for the rise of photography and the decline of illustration—although the two would cohabit on magazine pages for the next two decades. Baron de Meyer had moved over to *Harper's Bazaar* but Steichen's modernist leanings soon became the prevailing style of fashion photography. Nast and *Harper's Bazaar* owner William Randolph Hearst fiercely competed with each other as fashion illustrators, and increasingly fashion photographers, switched allegiances between the two giants—a dance that continues to this day. During the 1920s, a boom time for fashion and fashion magazines, fashion editor Carmel Snow, worked closely with Steichen, and is widely credited with bringing fashion photography into the modernist period. Their sleek and dramatically lit Art Deco inspired fashion shoots—frequently featuring American beauties such as Marion Moorehouse and Lee Miller in the latest models by Chanel,

Dorothy Shaver *(center)*, *Top*
Carmel Snow and Alexey
Brodovitch, 1952 *Bottom*

Augustabernard, Poiret, Vionnet, and the rest of the crème de la crème of Paris designers. Likewise, Hollywood blossomed as a major force in American culture during the 1920s, and fashion magazines increasingly blended images of these new movie stars into their editorial coverage. Cecil Beaton and Georges Hoyningen-Huene's theatrical and artistic photos increased the glamour of fashion magazines inspired by movies, the ballet, and avant-garde artistic trends. In fact many of the photographers of the period were trained artists or artisans, picking up the camera more for the career opportunities it offered, rather than, artistic aspirations.

The shock of the stock-market crash of 1929 put Parisian fashions out of reach for all but the very rich in America. The arrival of sound motion pictures the next year as well as radio gave Americans new entertainment options far from Broadway. The extravagant productions that Hollywood churned out included work by seminal costume designers such as Edith Head and Gilbert Adrian whose designs for stars like Katharine Hepburn and Greta Garbo captivated American women and profoundly influenced other fashion designers. Meanwhile in New York, important editors such as Edna Chase and merchandisers such as Dorothy Shaver at Lord & Taylor began to nurture the national fashion industry, increasingly promoting its designers by name. While men dominated French fashion, women designers topped the men during the 1930s in the New York fashion world. The development of sportswear and play clothing by pioneers such as Clare Potter and Claire McCardell were complemented by the dressier custom clothes by talents such as Elizabeth Hawes, Muriel King, and Valentina. The era also saw the emergence of a host of American female fashion photographers such as Toni Frissell and Louise Dahl-Wolfe.

The biggest American fashion moment of the 1930s was on the other side of the pond, however, as the scandal and the subsequent abdication of Edward VIII to wed American divorcée Wallis Warfield Simpson unfolded. When American-born Mainbocher, working in Paris during the decade, designed the soon-to-be Duchess of Windsor's wedding dress in "Wallis Blue" for the 1937 wedding, photos by Cecil Beaton and others were published in newspapers and magazines throughout the world.

When the United States entered World War II in 1941, floods of talented artists and designers sought refuge in New York and Hollywood. While widely believed to have been shut down completely during Nazi occupation, many French fashion houses and their related industries, it was later learned, remained open at least marginally—though American buyers and designers were cut-off from their influence. This turned out to be a boon to American fashion creativity, as designers came to rely more on their native talents. The L-85 regulations imposed on traditional material such as leather, wool, and silk would also propel, rather than hinder, designers in New York and Hollywood who worked within the regulations with wit and imagination.

Fashion publicist Eleanor Lambert became a driving force in the promotion of American fashion, launching influential publicity vehicles such as the International Best Dressed List in 1940 and representing individual designers and arranging fashion shows and press events throughout the war.

John Fairchild, 1967 *Top*

Carrie Donovan 1965 *Bottom*

Anthony Mazzola, 2005 *Top*
Diana Vreeland, 1989 *Middle*
Grace Mirabella, 1989 *Bottom*

Just after the war, in 1946, Parisian couturiers sent a novel advertisement—a traveling benefit war-relief exhibition called *Theatre de la Mode*—to American buyers, announcing that fashion in Paris was still very much alive. Comprised of dozens of wire dolls dressed in clothes by leading Parisian designers and featured in tableaus by a host of Paris-based artists, it was an influential harbinger of the upcoming return of Parisian fashion: the next year, Christian Dior launched his revolutionary New Look.

While American buyers and editors flocked back to Paris with abandon, the expanding American fashion industry now rested on a more established foundation. The prosperity of the 1950s and the rise of suburban culture as the prevailing lifestyle, with its reliance on the automobile and time-saving appliances, found a broad sector of American women returning to a more domestic life. An equally large share joined the workforce—a dichotomy that could be seen in the two opposing stereotypes of the era: the June Cleaver/Lucille Ball all-American stay-at-home mothers and at the other end of the spectrum, the worldlier, sexier, independent Marilyn Monroe/Ava Gardner types. In fashion terms, it was a contrast between suburban car coats and the urban, New Look–inspired evening gowns and cocktail attire. The Cold War emphasis on conformity also pervaded the fashions of the era. During the 1950s, while many others were overshadowed by the manufacturers or department stores they worked for, American designers such as Mainbocher, Norman Norell, Pauline Trigère, Arnold Scaasi, and Luis Estévez increasingly became known by name.

Jacqueline Kennedy's arrival on the scene as First Lady in 1961 and Diana Vreeland's appointment the next year as editor-in-chief of *Vogue* did much to spread American fashion across the map. Urged by fashion leaders such as Eleanor Lambert to unite, the CFDA was founded to protect and promote the original work of American fashion designers—with Sydney Wragge as its first president. The affordability of air travel and the youth culture of the 1960s transformed American fashion once again. Fashion flowered on the East and West Coasts, and designers such as Bill Blass, Oscar de la Renta, Geoffrey Beene, and Oleg Cassini all became well-known designers throughout America during the 1960s. By the time America entered the 1970s, the extravagant fantasies of bohemian chic and the Pop art–inspired grooves of the downtown boutique trends seemed decidedly passé. Grace Mirabella took the helm from Vreeland at *Vogue*, ushering in the era of the new American woman, while art director Anthony Mazzola took the helm at *Harper's Bazaar*.

Fashion and lifestyle moved to a more natural and casual stance, and this sense of minimalism was captured in the collections of Halston, Calvin Klein, Giorgio Sant'Angelo, Perry Ellis, Anne Klein's designers Donna Karan and Louis Dell'Ollio, Diane von Furstenberg, and Mary McFadden. In 1973, Eleanor Lambert coupled five American designers with five French designers for a benefit fashion show at the palace of Versailles outside of Paris. It was a watershed moment for American fashion as its creators announced their arrival on the world stage. The emotional drag of the Vietnam War, Watergate, the oil crisis, and finally the Iran hostage situation had taken its toll. But as the decade came to a close, America, and American fashion, discarded its beige demeanor in favor of the bright lights of disco and glamour.

The arrival of the Reagans in the White House in 1981 solidified the rapid reversal of tastes from the 1970s, with Americans celebrating power and wealth. During the 1980s, American fashion saw an explosion of talent as individual designers became brand names. The first instances of this were thanks to department stores like Bloomingdale's, who created in-store designer boutiques and large-scale advertising and promotion campaigns for designers such as Calvin Klein and Ralph Lauren. Those successes led to designers opening their own retail outlets, designing new lines and licensing fragrances and other products. In the 1990s, the unparalleled influence of telecommunications, technology, and the Internet lifted American fashion onto a truly global plane. American designers took the helm at major European fashion houses—underscoring the extraordinary reach American fashion had accomplished. Another major influence on fashion in America over the past three decades is Anna Wintour, the editor-in-chief of American *Vogue* since 1988. She has been a prominent force in the industry, with both her creative fashion editorial work and her keen eye for fashion trends. She is responsible for the establishment of the CFDA/Vogue Fashion Fund, an unprecedented initiative to aid emerging American fashion designers struggling to build successful businesses.

In the new millennium, American fashion is world fashion, and its designers are as well known at home as they are abroad. *American Fashion*, commissioned by the CFDA to celebrate that history, energetically illustrates the upward crescendo and extraordinary accomplishment that American fashion designers have worked toward and achieved the world over. These seven chapters are meant as flexible epochs anchored by key moments of American fashion history. As any student of history knows, societal and artistic changes do not fall into place in an orderly fashion. While decades are convenient ways of speaking of particular eras, they are not without their own inherent weaknesses. The period between the Crash of 1929 and the beginnings of World War II, for example, is a more sensible parameter than, say, the 1930s versus the 1940s. Likewise, the years between Dior's New Look in 1947 and the arrival of the Kennedys in the White House in 1961 seem like a logical time span, and the exit of Diana Vreeland and the Versailles fashion show in 1973 bounded by the beginning of the Reagan era in 1981 has its own rationale and logic. So great were the changes during the 1980s and 1990s, and with so many of the same designers active during those decades that it felt more exigent to tell the story of American fashion's rise to global power through the lens of those remarkable decades seen together.

Finally, the life-changing ramifications of September 11 certainly were a turning point of global proportions that we are still dealing with today. We conclude this book by focusing on both the new talents shaping American fashion's future as well as the already established, internationally known American designers whose global presence continues to expand the thriving creative and economic power of the American fashion industry. In all its originality and individuality, American fashion is a mirror of our own national image and its history—a heritage that bears repeating.

Anna Wintour, 2007 *Top*

Glenda Bailey, 2007 *Bottom*

Ceil Chapman, 1949
Opposite Cecil Beaton created a Matisse-inspired backdrop for Chapman's New Look inspired evening ensembles. On the left is her high collar cape over a floral print Swiss organdie dress and, on the right, a grey rayon taffeta coat with a net Pierrot collar over a matching taffeta and net dinner dress.

Versailles, 1973
Following pages Helmut Newton captures the historical presentation of American fashion at Versailles.

1933 Revelers celebrate the end of Prohibition

With the stock-market crash of October 29, 1929, America entered the Great Depression, a period of economic struggle that would only be compounded by escalating tensions in Europe. As annual incomes for the American family plummeted by an average of 40 percent, from $2,300 to $1,500 per year, thousands traversed the Dust Bowl in search of agricultural work. In 1933, Franklin Roosevelt's ascendancy to the presidency and his promise of a "New Deal" saw the implementation of government agencies, regulations, and commissions to reverse the country's dire economic woes. The Work Projects Administration (WPA), established in 1935, employed millions of American workers across the country, and the Social Security Act (1935) guaranteed income for elderly Americans. At the same time, workers became increasingly aware of their rights, forming unions such as the Congress of Industrial Organizations (CIO). Perhaps to give a bit of relief in these trying times, the Volstead Act, which had banned the manufacture, transportation, and sale of intoxicating liquors in America since 1919, was repealed in 1933.

Across the Atlantic, democratic governments in Spain, German, and Italy fell to dictatorships, fueling the rise of fascism throughout the world. As Hitler threatened to expand Germany's domain, American political thought continued to caution against intervention in the war. Thanks to WPA programs, American art flourished: Both the Museum of Modern Art and the Whitney Museum of American Art opened in New York during the early '30s. With funds supplied in part by the WPA, sculptor Gutzon Borglum continued to labor on his enormous Mount Rushmore Memorial in South Dakota, while San Francisco's Golden Gate Bridge opened in 1937. Despite the country's economic ills, several landmarks of American architecture were completed, including New York's Empire State and Chrysler Buildings, and Frank Lloyd Wright's Fallingwater, outside Pittsburgh.

On the literary scene, American novelists Ernest Hemingway and Thornton Wilder, as well as poets Carl Sandburg and Wallace Stevens, were among the brightest stars. Broadway produced some its most enduring musicals by legends such as George and Ira Gershwin, Cole Porter, Irving Berlin, and Richard Rogers, and big bands led by Duke Ellington and Glenn Miller filled the airwaves and dance halls. As it entered the era of sound in 1931, Hollywood would help America forget its troubles.

1935 Photographer Martin Munkásci captures the quintessential American family

1937 Aviator Amelia Earhart disappears in the Pacific

1934 Cole Porter composes the score to *Anything Goes*

1933 Eleanor Roosevelt, First Lady and American fashion supporter

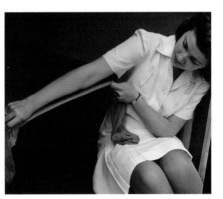

1938 Nylon stockings are introduced to the market

1930s Americans suffer through the Great Depression

CA.1939 *Vogue* editor (1914–1952) Edna Woolman Chase broadcasts on the radio

21

In 1938 singer Kate Smith first introduced Irving Berlin's "God Bless America," a song that would become an anthem during World War II and forever afterward. After Germany invaded Poland on September 1, 1939, British prime minister Neville Chamberlain declared war. At first, the United States was hesitant to take up arms, limiting aid to humanitarian efforts. But Japan's bombing of Pearl Harbor on December 7, 1941, shattered America's isolationist policies, and by 1942 the world was at war, with the Allied powers, led by the United States, Great Britain, and the Soviet Union, pitted against the Axis powers, led by Germany, Italy, and Japan. As President Franklin D. Roosevelt guided the country on the home front, Dwight D. Eisenhower commanded the troops in Europe. After the U.S. dropped the first two atomic bombs on the Japanese cities of Hiroshima and Nagasaki, Japan surrendered and President Harry S. Truman proclaimed victory on May 8, 1945. In the following months, the world would come to grasp the magnitude of Hitler's Holocaust, as concentration camps were liberated and the extermination of more than 6 million Jews, Gypsies, homosexuals, and the handicapped was revealed. In all, more than 70 million people were killed.

In the late '30s and early '40s, a wave of émigrés from all over Europe fled to the U.S. in search of asylum. In addition to book burnings and other forms of harassment of artists and intellectuals, Hitler's Third Reich deemed modern European art "degenerate" and confiscated and destroyed tens of thousands of works. Artists such as Willem de Kooning, Franz Kline, Piet Mondrian, Arshile Gorky, Adolph Gottlieb, and Hans Hofmann would all make New York their home during the war, and would influence the development of abstract painting that came to full flower in the '50s.

In American literature, Richard Wright's *Native Son*, addressing racial prejudice, and John Steinbeck's *The Grapes of Wrath*, chronicling the misery of life in the Dust Bowl, were two of the era's most influential books. Hollywood also joined the war effort; Michael Curtiz's *Casablanca* (1942) and Orson Welles's *Citizen Kane* (1941) were released and many stars enlisted or entertained troops abroad. Pinup stars like Betty Grable and Rita Hayworth became iconic, as did Rosie the Riveter—a fictional symbol of the thousands of American women who had joined the workforce. And in 1939 and 1940, over 45 million people visited the World's Fair in New York and got their first glimpse of that all-American icon, the television.

1940 Women enter the workforce in record numbers

1942 Zoot Suit Riots erupt in Los Angeles, CA

1942 *Casablanca* premieres

1942 Rosie the Riveter gives inspiration to working women

1941 FDR announces America's entry into World War II

1946 The first modern-style bikini debuts in Paris

1942 Louise Dahl-Wolfe shoots at Frank Lloyd Wright's Taliesin, Arizona

1945 President Truman drops the atomic bomb

1945 America honors its fallen heroes after the end of World War II

1943 Fashion becomes patriotic as *Vogue* uses a flag factory as a backdrop

1947/1960

1951 Americans tune into television

Jubilation over victory in World War II soon dimmed, as the capitalist United States and communist Soviet Union were increasingly at odds concerning postwar security around the globe. It was a period of great tension between the U.S. and the Russians, and percolated with increasing rhetorical spin. The dangers of the Cold War would last for decades, as Americans built bomb shelters and practiced emergency preparedness. In 1949, Mao Tse Tung defeated the U.S.-backed Kuomintang regime in China, leading to a seismic shift in the balance of power in Asia; the Korean War (1950–1953) was one of these instances. But even as war raged in Korea, the Marshall Plan for the rebuilding of Europe supplied billions in economic aid to Western Europe. The death of Joseph Stalin in 1953 and rise of Nikita Khrushchev pitted the fervently anticommunist supporters of President Dwight D. Eisenhower against Khrushchev's expanding Soviet empire. As the countries pointed nuclear weapons in each other's direction, the situation became increasingly threatening.

In 1947, the House Committee on Un-American Activities (HUAC) took Hollywood to task, holding nine days of hearings in Washington that led to the "blacklisting" of hundreds of film directors and actors either for their alleged communist sympathies or for their failure to name others. Senator Joseph McCarthy's reckless accusations culminated in 1954. That same year, the landmark case of Brown v. Board of Education officially banned segregation in public schools and helped to inspire the modern civil rights movement led by Reverend Martin Luther King, Jr. The passage of the Federal-Aid Highway Act of 1956 ushered in the interstate system crisscrossing the country as more and more single-family housing units were built, spreading suburban culture.

On a lighter note, television programs such as *I Love Lucy* and *The Honeymooners* and vaudeville stars like Milton Berle and Jack Benny entertained America. The "Beat" poets and writers—Allen Ginsberg, Lawrence Ferlinghetti, Jack Kerouac, and William Burroughs—broke onto the scene with their anti-Establishment voices, while African American writers such as Lorraine Hansbury, Langston Hughes, and James Baldwin made notable literary contributions. As their parents hummed along to Nat King Cole and Frank Sinatra, teenagers became obsessed with the gyrations and bold rock-and-roll of Elvis Presley and Chuck Berry.

1955 James Dean stars in *Rebel Without a Cause* and dies the same year

1959 Doris Day and Rock Hudson star in the film *Pillow Talk*

1955 National Highway Act builds the interstate road system

1951 Jackson Pollock becomes the best known artist of the New York School

1956 Elvis Presley releases his *Heartbreak Hotel*

1957 Audrey Hepburn and Fred Astaire appear in the musical *Funny Face* inspired by Richard Avedon

1955 Marilyn Monroe stars in *The Seven Year Itch*

1947 Lauren Bacall and Humphrey Bogart lead a protest of the hearings held by HUAC

For many Americans, the early 1960s marked a time of innocence and optimism. The thousand days of "Camelot," presided over by the young and charismatic John and Jacqueline Kennedy, would be cut short with Kennedy's assassination on November 22, 1963. From this date, the cultural tide turned from the conservative 1950s to the revolutionary 1960s. During the Kennedy and Johnson administrations, America became more deeply involved in the civil war in Vietnam. The institution of the military draft in 1965 further polarized the country, as the children of the baby boom were coming of age and wanted a far more liberal society than that of their parents. Lyndon Johnson's Great Society initiatives and civil rights legislation helped to fuel the debate on strategies of change, ranging from the radicalism of Malcolm X to the nonviolent demonstrations led by Martin Luther King, Jr.

The assassinations of Malcolm X in 1965 and Martin Luther King, Jr. as well as presidential candidate Robert F. Kennedy in 1968, cast a pall over American spirits. By the late '60s, as political and civil rights riots continued to spread across the country, the violence reached a breaking point, culminating with mass arrests at the 1968 Democratic Convention in Chicago and the deadly shootings of students at Kent State University in Ohio in 1970. President Johnson's decision not to run for reelection, and the election of Richard Nixon in 1968, only added to polarizing sides of political thought during the era.

Politics wasn't the only place of evolution and rebellion. The arrival of the Beatles in 1964 set off a music revolution that had been gathering steam in the early rock-and-roll of the 1950s. The counterculture musical styles of Janis Joplin, Jimmy Hendrix, and the Rolling Stones, along with the folk influence of Joni Mitchell and Bob Dylan, would inform young American tastes as the decade progressed. In 1969, the hippie movement of long-haired abandon and free love dominated in the Woodstock Festival, a four-day music extravaganza.

Reflecting changing social trends, the counter culture espoused by people like Timothy Leary called for Americans to drop out of Establishment society and to tune in to the psychedelic world of drugs. Andy Warhol, Robert Rauschenberg, Jasper Johns, and other visionaries heralded the ascendancy of American art, as New York replaced Paris as the international center of the art world.

1963 Martin Luther King, Jr. fights for civil rights

1962 Jacqueline Kennedy becomes America's fashion ambassador

1969 Apollo XI lands on the moon

1970 Ali MacGraw and Ryan O'Neal star in *Love Story*

1969 Peter Fonda and Dennis Hopper star in *Easy Rider*

1968 Andy Warhol becomes Pop Art's best known artist

1969 Santana and other music legends perform at Woodstock

1965 The Paraphernalia clothing boutique opens in Manhattan

1967 Raquel Welch entertains soldiers in Vietnam

1968 Americans protest the Vietnam War

1972/1980

1977 Liza Minnelli and Mikhail Baryshnikov dance the night away at Studio 54

The United States underwent profound changes during the 1970s. In 1973, Vice President Spiro Agnew resigned amid scandal, only to be followed by President Nixon on August 9, 1974, after the revelations of the Watergate scandal threatened his impeachment. Vice President Gerald Ford took office and led the country in the bicentennial celebration of the Declaration of Independence in 1976. But many saw little cause for celebration: the Vietnam War continued to divide the country, even after the Paris Peace Accords initiated the withdrawal of U.S. military participation in 1973. Another divisive issue came to the forefront of national attention in 1973, when the Supreme Court legalized abortion through the decision of Roe v. Wade.

The face of America was changing. Increased immigration followed after the passing of the Immigration Act of 1965, which reformed a policy that favored Western Europeans. As a result, increasing numbers of people from Third World countries came to the U.S. during the 1970s. Gay and civil rights became mainstream issues, and women expanded their involvement in politics, winning notable seats in Congress and in state and municipal governments. By 1979, women had surpassed men in college enrollment for the first time. As minorities and women asserted their rights to jobs and education, affirmative action became a controversial policy and divorce rates soared.

On the small screen, sitcoms like *All in the Family*, *Maude*, and *The Jeffersons* broke new ground in television programming by using controversial issues of the day as their subject matter. For those in search of easy laughs, comedy and variety shows such as *The Carol Burnett Show*, *The Flip Wilson Show*, *The Sonny & Cher Comedy Hour*, and NBC's *Saturday Night Live* were major hits. Many of the defining literary works of the 1970s were subsequently made into Hollywood films including: Erich Segal's *Love Story*, Judith Rossner's *Looking for Mr. Goodbar*, Stephen King's *The Shining*, William Styron's *Sophie's Choice*, and Tom Wolfe's *The Right Stuff*. In the sports arena, the country's "Battle of the Sexes" was exemplified by the 1973 tennis match between Billie Jean King and Bobby Riggs; King's defeat of her chauvinist challenger brought an enthusiastic, wider audience for women's sports across many fields. And perhaps as a sign of this tumultuous period, the decade culminated with a bang, when the long-dormant Mount St. Helens volcano erupted on May 18, 1980.

1974   Muhammad Ali defeats George Foreman and regains his heavyweight title

1977   *Saturday Night Fever* premieres starring John Travolta

1976   The United States celebrates the Bicentennial of the Declaration of Independence

1972   Antiwar protests surge to the forefront

1977   Woody Allen and Diane Keaton star in *Annie Hall*

1976   ABC debuts *Charlie's Angels*

1974   President Richard Nixon resigns

The 1980s and 1990s saw the world move from the industrial age to the information age. Compact discs, the Walkman, VHS recorders, fax machines, mobile phones, and personal computers would all impact communication, lifestyle, and business. On the political front, Ronald Reagan's two-term presidency marked a time of economic prosperity for many Americans, although his cuts to social services and his administration's failure to confront the AIDS pandemic were blights on his record. Reagan did much to raise the rhetoric and tensions between the United States and the Soviet Union, rekindling Cold War animosities, as well as launching costly defense initiatives. The rise of Mikhail Gorbachev as the last leader of the Soviet Union, with his modernizing policies of reform, led to a gradual easing of tensions. Technological advances played a role as well as it became harder to control the flow of communication that the computer age had engendered. Over the course of the decade, Reagan and Gorbachev's relations improved, as the days of communist Russia were numbered: the Berlin Wall fell in 1989, and the Soviet Union was dissolved 1991.

George H. W. Bush's presidency witnessed a massive economic decline, a military intervention in Nicaragua, and the first Persian Gulf War in 1991. The election of President Bill Clinton turned the tide as he presided over the longest peacetime growth in American economic history, finishing his second term with a balanced budget and a federal tax surplus, though his tenure was compromised by an alleged affair with a White House intern.

For Americans in the '80s and early '90s, working out, celebrity-endorsed aerobics routines, and a litany of faddish diets were popular obsessions. Cigarette smoking came under fire, while recreational and prescription drug usage soared. New Wave and pop music gave way to Generation X–inspired grunge from bands like Nirvana, the rap and hip-hop music of Tupac Shakur, and the rise in popularity of Latin music. Stars like Michael Jackson and Madonna took advantage of the MTV-led music video revolution, and talk shows multiplied as viewers tuned in to David Letterman, Phil Donahue, and Oprah Winfrey. *Miami Vice* and other television series of the 1980s gave way to more opulent evening soap operas such as *Dynasty* and *Dallas,* and sitcoms like *Cheers* and *Seinfeld* helped define the era. On the big screen, science fiction and action films abounded, from *E.T.* and *Star Wars* to *Rocky* and *The Terminator*.

1993 Bill and Hillary Clinton move into the White House

1981 MTV launches the first music television network

1987 ACT UP (The AIDS Coalition to Unleash Power) forms in New York City

1985 Donna Karan designs her first women's collection

1981 Michael Jackson's *Thriller* is released

1981 *Dynasty* airs on ABC

1994 Rock guitarist Kurt Cobain commits suicide

1989 The Berlin Wall falls

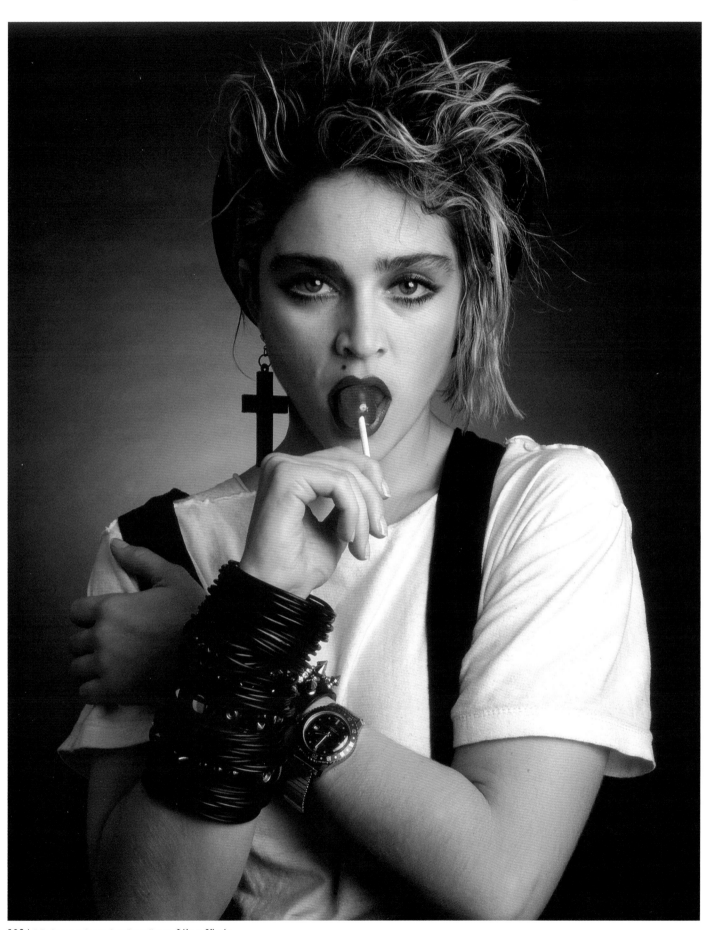

1984 Madonna releases her first album, *Like a Virgin*

2000...

2003 "Towers of Light" memorialize the twin towers of the World Trade Center

The time leading up to the millennium was one of retrospection and anticipation. Virtually all media focused on recalling the key moments, trends, and events of a century that was extraordinarily colorful and creative but bleak and deadly as well. The wired world of the 1990s, which had come to rely on computer technology and the World Wide Web, faced the threat of a super computer virus dubbed Y2K. But for the most part, the world ushered in the new millennium with little drama save for lavish celebrations. In American political life, controversy soared when the outcome of the 2000 presidential election was called into question.

Although George W. Bush lost the popular vote, the Supreme Court awarded him the necessary electoral votes, leading Al Gore to concede defeat. The life-changing events surrounding September 11, 2001, thrust the United States into the era of terrorism, causing a seismic global transformation of contemporary life. Declaring a "War on Terrorism," the Bush Administration convinced Congress that both Afghanistan, under the Taliban and Osama bin Laden's Al Qaeda network as well as Iraq, under dictator Saddam Hussein, posed a potentially cataclysmic threat to U.S. security. In March 2003, Congress gave Bush a mandate to invade Afghanistan and Iraq based on United Nations Resolution 1441. The War on Terrorism has proved controversial and divisive both in America and around the world, with the deaths of thousands of U.S.-led coalition soldiers, as well as untold numbers of Afghan and Iraqi citizens.

The world, it seemed, continued to become a smaller place, as disasters affected people across the globe. Earthquakes, the devastating 2004 tsunami in the Indian Ocean, the SARS and Avian flu epidemics, and, in the U.S., Hurricane Katrina, were just a few of the crises that challenged the world in the years just after the turn of the century. Global warming and other environmental concerns drew increasing attention. Apple's introduction of the iPod in 2001 revolutionized the portable entertainment industry. Reality TV shows such as *Survivor* and *American Idol* took an increasingly wider share of the television audience, and Web-based communications continued to expand with the popularity of blogs and sites like YouTube.

2006 Pope John Paul II dies

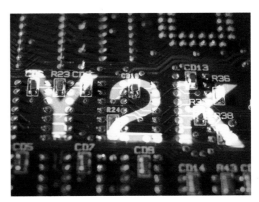
2000 The world marks a new millenium

2002 *Sex and the City* brings big city fashion to America

2005 Lance Armstrong wins the Tour de France for the seventh consecutive time

2003 The U.S. led coalition topples Iraq's Saddam Hussein

2001 Apple introduces the iPod

2006 Vice President Al Gore brings heightened awareness to ecological issues

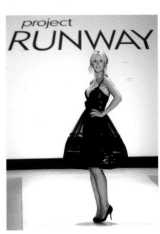
2004 *Project Runway* premieres

1929/1938

Dramatic Beginnings

HOLLYWOOD AND NEW YORK DESIGNERS BRING LUXURY AND SPORT TO DEPRESSION-ERA AMERICA

Elizabeth Hawes, 1932
Opposite Katharine Hepburn, fresh from her first box office hit—George Cukor's *A Bill of Divorcement* (1932), with John Barrymore—wears a black Hawes couture gown for *Harper's Bazaar.*

Travis Banton, 1934
Previous pages *Vogue* colorized Georges Hoyningen-Huene's black-and-white photo of actress Miriam Hopkins, starring that year in Rouben Mamoulian's *Becky Sharp*—the first Hollywood film in Technicolor.

On October 24, 1929, the fashionable hemlines that had inched their way up the legs of fun-loving flappers during the hectic 1920s took a dramatic fall: the Great Depression had arrived. The styles personified by young, androgynous bobbed-haired girls and their all-American heartthrobs vanished seemingly overnight. The Roaring Twenties, epitomized by stars like silent film icon Louise Brooks and crooner Rudy Vallee, was now over.

Despite the gloom that shadowed the 1930s, there was a silver lining. The new icons of style were dance partners Fred Astaire and Ginger Rogers, who captivated the country with their musical films: Rogers with a more formal and feminine style that played between tailored and sleek, swanky and ornamental; Astaire representing the epitome of the modern well-dressed American man. The look of 1930s men's and women's clothing remains today a standard of elegance that designers return to and draw inspiration from. And a talented pool of native-born and émigré American designers was rising to prominence, not only to the credit of their own formidable talents but also because of the revolution in mass media and communications. These developments, particularly sound motion pictures and radio, allowed fashion to first be promoted on a national stage.

The grim economic truths of 1930s America however afforded designers an unexpected benefit—a greater demand for domestic clothing. Paris fashion may still have reigned critically, but the fact was that imported fashion was simply too expensive for all but the very rich. Also working in favor of these emerging designers was the reality that dressing up was now serious business. Men and women of society regularly attended formal opening nights at the theater, and dressing glamorously was *de rigueur*. The proper wardrobe included day-and evening-wear ensembles for luncheon, teatime, cocktails and charity balls, as well as Broadway and Hollywood premieres—which spread the era's fashionable styles across the country in big cities and small towns alike. New stars of entertainment—as well as the society figures that befriended them—came together at fashionable restaurants and nightclubs in a heady blend that came to be known as Café Society.

Such glamorous couples as *Time* magazine's founder Henry Luce and his fashionable wife, Clare Boothe Luce (a former *Vanity Fair* editor and author who also penned the 1930s hit play *The Women*), mingled at hotspots like the

Travis Banton, 1936

As Paramount's chief designer during the 1930s, Banton helped shape the look and images of such stars as Carole Lombard, Mae West, and later on, Rita Hayworth. Marlene Dietrich, who played Catherine the Great in Josef von Sternberg's *The Scarlet Empress* in 1934, wears a black velvet coat ornately embroidered with swirls of white.

El Morocco and the Ritz's Lark Room. Gathering nightly were the best-known artists and talents of the day, among them composer Cole Porter, artist Salvador Dalí, American theater's Alfred Lunt and Lynn Fontanne, and the dozens of British stars who crossed the Atlantic to work on Broadway and in Hollywood, such as Noël Coward and Gertrude Lawrence. Their international master of ceremonies was the indefatigable party giver Elsa Maxwell. When *Vogue* publisher Condé Nast threw a party in 1938 for the cast of *The Women*, he recorded a guest list of almost 900 people with two orchestras entertaining the throng.

Café Society also embraced the excitement of the Harlem Renaissance, rushing uptown to the Apollo Theater, in white tie and ball dress, to catch the latest show. Though racial prejudices continued to abound, the 1930s saw the emergence of African-American performers moving into mainstream entertainment, such as Josephine Baker, who reigned as the toast of Paris. All black casts of the Virgil Thomson/Gertrude Stein opera *Four Saints in Three Acts* (1934) and Gershwin's *Porgy and Bess* (1935) broke major new ground, as did Paul Robeson's appearances in London in *Show Boat* (1928) and in the film version of Eugene O'Neill's *The Emperor Jones* (1933). Singers as diverse as Mabel Mercer and opera's Marian Anderson, together with many others, began to erode racial boundaries in popular culture.

Also moving in these circles were some of the best-dressed figures of the day, among them America's Mrs. Harrison Williams (later known as Mona Bismarck), Singer sewing-machine heiress Mrs. Reginald (Daisy) Fellowes, and younger heiresses and fashion plates, such as Barbara Hutton of the Woolworth fortune and tobacco heiress Doris Duke. Mixing with European nobles, artists, actors, and other colorful personalities, they captured the public's attention with their mode of dress and lifestyle—all put into print by columnists such as Walter Winchell and Hedda Hopper, who reported on their antics daily.

Fashion designers were garnering public interest, and in New York a brigade of new names emerged with the help of supporters like Lord & Taylor's legendary vice-president Dorothy Shaver. Beginning in 1932, Shaver was the first major retail executive to feature American designers by name in window and store displays as well as in advertisements. Other department stores, including Jay Thorpe, Bergdorf Goodman, and a host of elite specialty stores, followed Lord & Taylor's lead. Equally important were influential magazine editors such as Carmel Snow, Edna Woolman Chase, Bettina Ballard, Diana Vreeland, and Lois Long, as well as lesser-known but locally influential fashion editors writing in newspapers across the country. Together they helped popularize the fashionable looks of the day rising out of New York and Hollywood.

Another milestone in the history of American fashion during this decade was the establishment in 1930 of the Fashion Group (known today as Fashion Group International) by *Vogue's* influential Edna Chase. Among its founders were First Lady Eleanor Roosevelt, editors Carmel Snow and Jessica Daves, cosmetics queens Helena Rubinstein and Elizabeth Arden,

New York designers Lilly Daché, Clare Potter, Claire McCardell, Adele Simpson, and Hollywood's Edith Head. Together with the other imaginative designers of the era, these editors and retailers stimulated sales at every price point—instigating a rising prominence for the country's new fashion-design community.

Along with Edith Head, costume designers for Hollywood's biggest film studios, such as Gilbert Adrian (MGM) and Orry-Kelly (who worked for virtually all the major studios), as well as custom California designers such as Travis Banton and Howard Greer astonished filmgoers and magazine readers with their dazzling outfits for stars such as Marlene Dietrich, Katharine Hepburn, Greta Garbo, and Joan Crawford. It became clear that film stars could sell clothes, and magazines and movie studios soon collaborated with mutual benefit—a lucrative pairing that continues to this day. Tightening the bond, publisher Condé Nast became a board member of 20th Century Fox and even created a magazine called *Glamour of Hollywood* (later *Glamour*) in 1939.

Fashion retailing struck in full force as Adrian, based in California, opened specialty boutiques for custom and ready-to-wear clothing and offered his designs to leading department stores such as Saks Fifth Avenue. American women began to emulate their favorite stars. Hattie Carnegie, whose enormous New York–based specialty store employed a series of in-house designers, sold original and facsimile models of the most sought-after garments featured both on-screen and in the pages of fashion magazines. Macy's reported that it sold more than 50,000 copies of a dress Adrian designed for Joan Crawford for her 1932 film *Letty Lynton*.

At the same time, another style of clothing emerged in stark contrast with the glamour of Hollywood. Since the 1920s, American women had increasingly opted for ease and comfort in their leisure wear. Although pants, favored by Garbo, Dietrich, and Hepburn, failed to catch on in mainstream America until many years later, designers such as Clare Potter and Claire McCardell in New York and Tom Brigance in California began creating innovative sportswear that would grow in influence during and after World War II. All the while, and even though Paris couture still reigned supreme, the newly empowered American fashion community had achieved its own substantive boost. By the decade's end, American fashion designers were poised for a larger stage just as the veil of war began to descend across Europe.

Clare Potter, 1933
Opposite   Harper's Bazaar featured this 'Ladies' Doubles Gallery in White' reminding its readers that fashion does not exclude athletics.

Tom Brigance, 1939
Left   American designers were quick to embrace the new synthetic materials that were developed during the 1930s. Here a model dons a white rubber crepe one-piece bathing suit and matching bathing cap.

Valentina, 1936
Following page, left   The Russian-born designer opened her couture house in 1925 in New York, and stars of both Broadway and Hollywood came to her in droves. Actress Lynn Fontanne, seen here, was dressed by Valentina for Robert Sherwood's play *Idiot's Delight* that year.

Valentina, 1937
Following page, right   Japanese-American artist Isamu Noguchi, who studied with Constantin Brancusi in Paris, sketched this Valentina divided dress of heavy black silk. Gathered with elastic and drawn up to the knees in deep folds, it is worn with a conical hat draped with a long scarf—a signature Valentina look.

Bernard Weatherill Ltd., 1935

Above Katharine Hepburn prepares to take off from her native Hartford, Connecticut, in Weatherill's gray gabardine trousers, gray flannel coat, and white wool scarf—all custom designed. Although Hepburn, like Greta Garbo and Marlene Dietrich, embraced menswear in her professional and private life during the 1930s, it would be decades before American women followed their lead.

Howard Greer, 1935

Opposite Katharine Hepburn, nominated for an Academy Award in 1935 for her performance in *Alice Adams*, was one of the many celebrities whom Greer designed for at his custom clothing boutique in Los Angeles. Here, Hepburn wears a point d'esprit-over-pink satin blouse with a velvet skirt. She told *Harper's Bazaar,* "It is just the sort of dress for a girl like me with freckles and a long neck."

Gilbert Adrian, 1934

Above Adrian was Hollywood's most well-known designer during the 1930s and 1940s—credited with designs for over 250 films. Here, Martin Munkácsi captures Marion Davies at William R. Hearst's estate San Simeon, wearing a gown that Adrian designed for her for the 1933 film *Going Hollywood*.

Travis Banton, 1934

Opposite Carole Lombard starred with Gary Cooper and Shirley Temple in Henry Hathaway's *Now and Forever*, wearing a gown such as this gold lamé creation.

Jessie Franklin Turner/
Elizabeth Hawes, 1936
Opposite Hawes went to Paris in the
early 1930s and, while working in a couture
house, also penned a column on fashion
for *The New Yorker* under the nom de
plume Parasite. A sketch for *Vogue* features
both her own (right) and Turner's (left)
designs.

Elizabeth Hawes, ca. 1932
Left Jane Kendall Mason was the
inspiration for the lead character Margaret
Macomber in Ernest Hemingway's "The
Short Happy Life of Francis Macomber."
Here, on the eve of a Hemingway-led
safari in Africa, she wears a satin moiré
dress by Hawes.

Orry-Kelly, 1936

Right   Australian born Orry-Kelly's designs were featured in Busby Berkeley's extravagant *Gold Diggers of 1937*. Set just after the stock-market crash, and starring Dick Powell and Joan Blondell (center front), the film championed the notion that, despite all obstacles, the show must go on. Orry-Kelly worked for most of the major film studios until his death in 1964.

Muriel King, 1936

Following page, left   King, who began her career as an illustrator for *Vogue* and *Harper's Bazaar*, designed Ginger Rogers's costumes for the Edna Ferber/George S. Kaufman hit film *Stage Door*. King was one of the American designers first featured by Dorothy Shaver at Lord & Taylor in 1932.

Unknown, 1937

Following page, right   Fred Astaire remains, more than a half century hence, the epitome of the well-dressed American man.

Mainbocher, 1937

Below American divorcée Wallis Warfield Simpson became the most famous of the international best dressed after the abdication of Edward VIII in 1937 and her subsequent marriage to him in France. Here the newly wed and named Duke and Duchess of Windsor are captured by Cecil Beaton on their wedding day. Her ensemble is the creation of fellow American expatriate Mainbocher.

Charles James, 1936

Opposite James opened his first boutique in New York in 1928. Cecil Beaton's 1936 photograph for *Vogue* places a suite of James's opera capes within a surrealist trompe l'oeil setting.

Saks Fifth Avenue, 1938

Below and opposite In addition to the French couture it offered on a made-to-order basis, Saks had an in-house design business led by its owner's wife Sophie Gimbel, who began designing custom-made dresses in 1931, while Emmet Joyce designed Saks's ready-to-wear lines. Louise Dahl-Wolfe shot these now-iconic photos for *Harper's Bazaar*.

Hattie Carnegie, 1935

Right　Hattie Carnegie not only brought the couture collections of Schiaparelli and Chanel from Paris, she also imported hats—the quintessential 1930s accessory. In this image, actress Marion Davies's ensemble is topped with a turban by the leading Parisian milliner Agnés. Davies is dressed in Carnegie's ankle-length dinner dress of black satin.

Tom Brigance, ca. 1938

Opposite　Brigance, who served in World War II, designed this bathing suit and skirt for the Russian ballerina Irina Baronova for the Swedish tearjerker film *Florian*.

VOGUE

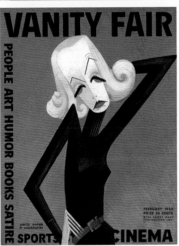

1939/1946

Wartime Invention and Expansion

THE WORLD IN FLAMES:
WARTIME LIMITATION
AND THE FLOWERING
OF AMERICAN FASHION

Lilly Daché, 1942

Opposite Daché, first known as a milliner, adjusted her designs during the war years to meet rations and suit the nation's sobriety. She launched her own clothing line in 1949.

Hattie Carnegie, ca. 1945

Previous pages The Duke of Windsor is credited for popularizing midnight blue as an alternative to black for men's dinner jackets. Here, Carnegie's twilight blue evening dress of rayon and cotton net is studded with star sequins.

It could be said that President Franklin D. Roosevelt reigned, rather than served, as America's president from 1933 until his death in 1945. For a generation born during the 1920s, he was the only president they had ever known. By the late 1930s, his New Deal policies and programs had begun to bear fruit—America seemed well on the road to economic recovery. Meanwhile, in 1939, Hollywood created two of its greatest cinematic wonders—*The Wizard of Oz* (costumed by Adrian) and *Gone with the Wind* (costumed by Walter Plunkett). But the threat of a deadly and far-reaching war, did much to overshadow those all too brief and shining moments. It was an ominous period where the question of American involvement in yet another world war pulled the country between isolation and intervention. That changed with the bombing of Pearl Harbor in December 1941, when Roosevelt declared war on Japan and soon after, the Axis powers in Europe. By the war's end, more than 70 million lives would be lost—and the world irrevocably altered.

When Paris fell to the Germans in 1940, the city's fashion houses were closed, only to reopen on the orders of Vichy's Marshall Pétain when he signed the armistice—though exports and profits were forbidden under Nazi rule. This allowed for expertise and craftsmanship to be preserved—though not perceived—by the American fashion-buying public. Freed of the dominating influence of Paris, designers in America were forced to rely on their own talents and resources, giving a new perspective to American fashion during the war years. The fashion industry, along with the motion-picture and broadcasting industries, became an integral part of the war effort as the country's resources and energies were redirected toward a common purpose. Fashion publications, once bastions of the frivolous, now featured well-heeled women dressed in uniform or cited particulars of their war work as volunteers and professionals. Patriotic styles abounded, from war-appropriate wardrobes for social and civil leaders to working clothes for women from all walks of life who joined the war effort.

Publicist Eleanor Lambert, who began representing fashion clients during the 1930s, became one of American fashion's greatest champions in the 1940s. During the war, she was joined by retail leaders Dorothy Shaver and Hattie Carnegie and magazine editors such as Edna Woolman Chase at

Vogue and Carmel Snow at *Harper's Bazaar*. Working on a national scale, in concert with American retailers and manufacturers, Lambert helped craft a publicity machine for American fashion that she would cultivate for decades to come. She coordinated press coverage of American designers, produced benefit fashions shows throughout the country, took on individual designers as clients, and was instrumental in the founding of the prestigious Coty Awards (1943–1984), given each year by the Fashion Critics of America. Other important leaders of American fashion during the war years included *New York Times* fashion writer Virginia Pope, whose "Fashion of the Times" columns would later evolve into the newspaper's magazine supplement. Sally Kirkland at *Life* and Lois Long at *The New Yorker* also championed American fashion. Ready-to-wear designer Maurice Rentner was the leader of an organization founded in 1932 called the Fashion Originators Guild—a pioneering group dedicated to protecting and promoting the original work of the country's top designers. In 1940, Lambert most famously created the International Best Dressed List, largely as a publicity ploy to promote the work of American designers as well as their glamorous customers. During the 1940s, the list included many fashionable American women, including Mrs. Harrison Williams (Mona Bismarck), Millicent Rogers, and Barbara Hutton. Younger fashionable American women also emerged into the spotlight, such as *Vogue* editors Barbara Cushing Mortimer (Babe Paley) and Babs Rawlings, and social fashion plates such as Gloria Vanderbilt and C. Z. Guest.

Another factor in the shaping of American fashion during the war years was a series of regulations known as the L-85. Issued by the United States War Production Board in December 1943 and periodically updated throughout the war, the L-85 specified the maximum yardage, dimensions, and details permitted in clothing manufacturing. Fabrics such as wool, silk, and leather were rationed and in some cases banned from nonmilitary use. The regulations also placed severe limits on changes to the prevailing boxy silhouette that characterized American tastes just before the war's outset. In doing so, the L-85 regulations eliminated the costly modifications to machinery that were necessary for the fluctuating styles of the previous decade. Rather than crippling American designers, the effects of the L-85 inspired them to work creatively within the regulations' fabric and manufacturing limitations. Their innovations and inventions impelled a flowering of native fashion design that would only be amplified in the following decade.

The leading American custom, or what came to be called "couture quality," designers during the war years were Valentina, Mainbocher (back from Paris), and Charles James. James, who had worked in Paris under Poiret in the 1930s, was hired to create a collection for Elizabeth Arden in 1941. But her collaboration with the temperamental James lasted for only one show. (James reopened under his own name in 1945.) Elizabeth Hawes retired from fashion design in 1940 but kept busy during the war, designing uniforms for the Red Cross volunteers, as well as writing for newspapers and

publishing her popular books on fashion and etiquette. Luxury retailers such as Hattie Carnegie and specialty stores such as Chez Ninon (where Jean Schlumberger, later celebrated for his jewelry, designed) were important advocates of American fashion, as were the country's leading department and specialty fashion stores. Ready-to-wear and sportswear designers such as Clare Potter and Claire McCardell, who had risen to prominence during the late 1930s, were joined by a bevy of talents including Ceil Chapman, Jo Copeland, Muriel King, Tina Leser, Vera Maxwell, Germaine Monteil, Norman Norell, Mollie Parnis, Pauline Potter, Nettie Rosenstein, Pauline Trigère, Emily Wilkens, and Sydney Wragge. Hollywood's Tom Brigance closed down in order to serve in the army, but his fellow Californians Adrian, Edith Head, Irene, Howard Greer, and a young Oleg Cassini (designing for Paramount before serving in the war) continued to influence and instill a dash of mid-century glamour, all the while respecting wartime regulations and material shortages.

American styles during the war years had a boxy and column-like simplicity, with exaggerated shoulder padding that mirrored the country's military posture. This evolving wartime style can be seen in the period's film noir classic *Mildred Pierce* (1945), for which Joan Crawford won an Academy Award. Warner Bros. costume designer Milo Anderson transformed Crawford's appearance during the course of the film from a soft and feminine housewife at the war's outset to a harsh and mannish, career-driven businesswoman at the war's end. The Crawford look was widely emulated.

The exotic foreign glamour of the 1930s, personified by Marlene Dietrich and Greta Garbo, gave way to the more natural, all-American beauty of the 1940s. Lauren Bacall's well-scrubbed and sultry poses in the numerous wartime fashion sittings that she did for both *Vogue* and *Harper's Bazaar* epitomize this wartime look. By war's end, the American fashion industry would have new challenges ahead as Paris fashion reasserted its influential force. The 1946 American tour of the *Theatre de la Mode*—dolls costumed by the leading French couturiers—beckoned the fashionable back to Paris. Christian Dior's revolutionary New Look in 1947, and the American fashion industry's excited response to it, marked the return of French fashion. But the inventions and innovations explored in American fashion during its period of isolation had established a firm footing for the future. The ensuing decade would further emancipate American designers, giving them a greater sense of freedom and providing a rich and fertile ground for a host of new talent on the American horizon.

Omar Kiam/Maurice Rentner, 1945

Above A showcase of spring wartime fashions: a shantung silk dress (right) by Omar Kiam for Ben Reig and a day suit (left) designed by Maurice Rentner, who headed America's Fashion Originators Guild—an early precursor to the CFDA. Kiam's and Rentner's designs are accented with hats by America's top milliners, John-Frederics and Lilly Daché, respectively.

Emily Wilkens, ca. 1945

Opposite Wilkens was one of the first American designers to create fashions for young women, rejecting the idea that their wardrobes should be derivative versions of the more mature styles worn by their mothers. In this wartime streetscape, *Vogue* coupled Wilkens's white rayon evening dress with green suede gloves.

Hattie Carnegie, 1946

Above Hattie Carnegie was one of the great powerhouses of American fashion from the mid-1920s to the 1960s. During World War II, her in-house custom designers included Jean Louis and Pauline Potter. Here, John Rawlings captures the first Mrs. William S. Paley, later known as Dorothy Hirshon, in a classic Carnegie suit ensemble.

Oleg Cassini, 1942

Opposite Parisian-born Cassini had just married actress Gene Tierney. He designed her costumes for the 1941 Josef von Sternberg film *The Shanghai Gesture*. Cassini initially joined the U.S. Coast Guard but later rose to second lieutenant in the U.S. Army. In time, Tierney exclusively relied on Cassini for her film costumes. They divorced in 1951.

Muriel King, 1943

Above King contributed to the war effort by designing coordinating outfits in "flight blue" for women aircraft workers. *Life* magazine featured actress Barbara Britton in one of King's industrial ensembles.

Valentina, 1940

Right The threat of war already loomed as a pensive Valentina modeled for *Harper's Bazaar* in her loose-woven linen dress accompanied by a straw hat tied with a handkerchief.

Clare Potter, 1944

Opposite The changing role of women in wartime is apparent in this gray cotton velveteen suit, sold at Bonwit Teller and "cut precisely like a mechanic's suit—slim, trim, and princely for evenings around the house," according to *Harper's Bazaar*.

Vera Maxwell, ca. 1944

Above Maxwell also designed uniforms for women working in the war effort and became known for her pared-down, economical design. Here, a model dons a camel-colored back-buttoned suit and cape.

Clare Potter, ca. 1943

Opposite John Rawlings captures the pensive but sophisticated cast of wartime fashion in this photograph of a model wearing Potter's natural-color mink coat draped over a platinum beige jumper dress with a blue and black diagonal neckline.

Lord & Taylor, ca. 1943

Previous pages Dorothy Shaver, a legendary promoter of American fashion designers, saluted American women in this wartime window display for Lord & Taylor.

Adrian, 1944

Opposite Man Ray captures Adrian's short black rayon crepe dinner dress with bands of white crepe knotted at the neck and hips, and cuffed at the top of the sleeves to leave the shoulders bare.

Tina Leser, 1940

Top When these models appeared in plaid sportswear, Tina Leser had already won both the Neiman Marcus and Coty awards. In 1935, she had opened a shop in Honolulu selling resort wear. Both *Vogue* and *Harper's Bazaar* touted Leser's sportswear.

Designer Unknown, 1941

Bottom A *Harper's Bazaar* photograph of a hand-knit black, wool sweater top and gold velvet skirt completed by a bolero cape, balloon muff, and wide amber-studded leopard belt. Hoyningen-Huene captures the model against a cubist masterpiece.

Hattie Carnegie, 1939
Above   Louise Dahl-Wolfe chose an eerily lifeless mannequin as the world went to war. The jewelry featured is by Paul Flato, who had outfitted Katharine Hepburn in George Cukor's film *Holiday* the year before.

Traina-Norell, 1943
Opposite   Louise Dahl-Wolfe captures wartime angst with glamour in Norman Norell's leopard ensemble, shot at Wildenstein Galleries in New York.

Clare Potter, ca. 1946
Following page, left   Initially an aspiring artist, by the 1940s Potter was well-known for both sportswear and evening clothes. Her classically inspired sand-colored jersey dinner dress with a fluted hemline is evidence of the designer's classic minimalist style.

Traina-Norell, 1946
Following page, right   Horst captures Mrs. Stanley Grafton Mortimer Jr. (later Babe Paley) in Traina-Norell's two-tone jersey gown. A *Vogue* editor and legendary beauty, Paley was one of the leading American fashion plates for decades.

Nettie Rosenstein, 1945

Bottom, left Lauren Bacall models Rosenstein's functional woolen coat featuring pockets for the woman on the move.

Adele Simpson, 1945

Bottom, right Before and after she became a screen star, Bacall appeared frequently in both *Vogue* and *Harper's Bazaar* in clothes by American designers. Here, Bacall wears Simpson's crepe blouse and black satin long skirt.

Carolyn Schnurer, 1946

Opposite During the war, a tour of South America inspired a complete fashion collection by Schnurer, which was seen in the best department stores across the country. Bacall models Schnurer's navy blue "playsuit" with a coverall coat.

Sydney Wragge, ca. 1946

Above B. H. Wragge was one of America's
most popular lines during the 1940s.
Dorian Leigh, one of the era's star models,
wears a pale pink cloche by Madame
Reine and Wragge's plunge-necked rayon
crepe dress.

Hi-Dee, 1945

Opposite Although Italian designer
Emilio Pucci is widely credited for starting
the rage for capri pants during the 1950s,
here we see them a decade earlier.
American fashion manufacturer Hi-Dee's
capri pants of mattress ticking with red
trim are paired with a sleeveless turtleneck
blouse. A patriotic ensemble for the active
wartime woman.

Larry Aldrich, ca. 1945

Previous page, left Although he had been a
clothing manufacturer since the 1920s,
Aldrich only started designing during the
1930s. By the 1940s, his simple, no-frills
outfits, such as this black-and-white
print dress with a rayon bow, reflected
the sober realities of wartime fashion, as
the newspaper's headline underscores.

Heller, ca. 1945

Previous page, right The wartime mood
pervaded American fashion magazines.
Here, a model dons Heller's black
turtleneck blouse and long green skirt
as her uniformed beau is lost in thought.

1947/1960

Back to the Future

POSTWAR NEW LOOKS FOR TOWN AND COUNTRY

The end of World War II ushered in profound changes for American society. Many women, who had taken on new jobs and became an important force in the war effort, moved back into domestic roles as their men returned home. Despite the period's stereotypical depictions in film and television of women as homemakers, they also entered the American workforce and attended colleges in ever expanding numbers. Gone with the depression and war was also the large pool of servants and other workers that had supported domestic life in America in more affluent, and less democratic times. Virtually every aspect of American life—from food preparation (the emergence of frozen and prepared foods) to dress (an increasing use of synthetic and wrinkle-free fabrics)—was transformed. Paris couture came back with renewed energy, due in large measure to Christian Dior and his revolutionary New Look of 1947.

American fashion editors and buyers flocked back to Paris with abandon, eager to rekindle their love affair with French couture. Even so, American designers had established a solid creative foundation during the war continuing to expand and flourish as they entered the postwar decade. Thanks to the increasing quality of American craftsmanship, and manufacturers' ability to produce and distribute American-designed ready-to-wear clothing, the consumerism that marked the era found designers gradually emerging out of anonymity. Fashion during this era reflected a new femininity—narrow upper bodices ballooned into long, full skirts of literally yards of fabric below tightly cinched wasp waists. While Dior gets most of the credit for this New Look, American designers such as Charles James, Mainbocher, Norman Norell, and Nettie Rosenstein also gave American women of the era the ultrafeminine and elaborate clothes (not always French-derived or -inspired) that they desired—and freed from the minimalism that wartime economies had necessitated. Irving Penn's iconic 1947 shot "Twelve Beauties" (featuring only American fashion) and Cecil Beaton's romantic 1948 grouping of Charles James-gowned beauties (both for *Vogue*) are ample evidence of this development. In Hollywood, Jean Louis's gowns for Rita Hayworth in films like *Gilda* (1946) reinforced a return to an American style of unabashed glamour that had not been seen since the 1930s.

While high-society entertaining and debutante rituals flourished, as America entered the 1950s, not every American woman spent her evenings in a ball gown. She was more likely to be cooking in her kitchen, minding children, or supervising her husband barbecuing on their suburban patio. The proliferation of couture quality and mass-produced American evening wear and sportswear, as well as the increasing demand for suitable working clothes, created a new American fashion client. It perfectly suited the expanding baby-boomer suburban culture that came to define the age. Factors in this cultural transformation included the enormous postwar home-building boom; the escalation of Cold War tensions and anxieties centered on the rivalry between the United States and the Soviet Union in a new atomic age; the expanding car culture impelled by the National Highway Act of 1956; and the proliferation of the medium of television, which kept Americans entertained in their new suburban homes. These cultural changes allowed Americans to forget the terrible war years and take advantage of affluent and optimistic times—even while bomb shelters were becoming *de rigueur* and Senator Joseph McCarthy ravenously hunted for Communists under every rock. Additionally, films like *The Man in the Gray Flannel Suit* (1956), starring Gregory Peck, portrayed the period's archetypal ambience of suburban conformity.

American women of the Cold War era had a kind of split personality. On one end of the spectrum were the conservative, stay-at-home, ladylike, good girl images promulgated by stars like Doris Day, and on the other end, the overtly sexy goddesses such as Marilyn Monroe and Ava Gardner who portrayed a more independent-minded modern woman. Seventh Avenue manufacturers retained enormous power over the field, however, failing to credit by name the large share of talents working for them. Bettina Ballard at *Vogue* and Carmel Snow and Diana Vreeland at *Harper's Bazaar* may have enthusiastically championed French fashion, but they also kept an eye on America's established designers as well as the emerging younger talents who were making innovative and highly wearable clothing for day, sport and evening. At both magazines, *Vogue*'s Alexander Liberman and *Harper's Bazaar*'s Alexey Brodovitch were influential art directors intent on shaking up magazine design—working closely with the era's top photographers, such as Richard Avedon, Irving Penn, John Rawlings, Erwin Blumenfeld, Henry Clarke, Louise Dahl-Wolfe, and Karen Radkai, to put a modern stamp on their publications. This mirrored the modernist trends in American art, architecture, and design that were increasingly embraced during the 1950s.

Larry Aldrich, Ceil Chapman, Charles James, Mainbocher, Norman Norell, Mollie Parnis, Nettie Rosenstein, Adele Simpson, Pauline Trigère, and Valentina were among the best known in the American market for luxurious day and evening wear. Both established and up-and-coming ready-to-wear designers expanded their influence and name recognition during the 1950s—thanks to the proliferation of an American fashion publicity machine driven by people like the formidable Eleanor Lambert

Larry Aldrich, 1957
Opposite Lauren Bacall wears a black two-piece ensemble in a rayon crepe, which was then available at Bonwit-Teller, Dayton's and Neiman Marcus.

Ferdinando Sarmi and Arnold Scaasi, ca. 1960
Following page, left Italian-born Sarmi was the in-house designer for Elizabeth Arden during the 1950s, dressing Pat Nixon for Eisenhower's inaugural in 1957. Bert Stern captured Sarmi's strapless, floor-length gown in silk chiffon with giant white carnation print (left) and Scaasi's strapless gown of white silk chiffon with matching fringed stole (right) for *Vogue*.

Gilbert Adrian, 1948
Following page, right After the war, Adrian's day and evening wear, such as this high-collar mauve cape and dress, continued to be coveted by fashionable women across the country.

and former–fashion editors Muriel Maxwell and Jane Gray. Both veteran and new designers to the scene took advantage of these promotions—garnering greater name recognition in the American fashion field. They included Tom Brigance, Bonnie Cashin, Oleg Cassini, Jo Copeland, Anne Fogarty, Anne Klein, Tina Leser, Clare Potter, Sophie of Saks, Sydney Wragge, and Ben Zuckerman. It would also be the end of the era for several pioneering American designers such as Hollywood's Adrian (retiring in 1952) and Valentina (1957). Ben Reig's Omar Kiam would die in 1954, followed by Hattie Carnegie in 1956 and Claire McCardell in 1958. In 1952, Jessica Daves became the third editor-in-chief in *Vogue's* history when Edna Chase retired.

The fertile landscape of custom and ready-made American clothing was blossoming during the 1950s. Thanks to cheaper air travel, many of the era's budding designers had apprenticed or studied for a time in Paris and/or worked with already established American designers in New York and California. Among them were Adolfo (first a hat designer), Geoffrey Beene, Bill Blass, Luis Estévez, James Galanos, Oscar de la Renta, Ferdinando Sarmi, and Arnold Scaasi.

The postwar era was one of enormous growth for American fashion—making the industry highly profitable during an incredibly affluent period. Designers and manufacturers began to branch out into other areas, including accessories of all kinds, children's clothing, early forays into menswear, as well as swimsuits and sports clothes. But many of the designers churning out fashion and accessories were intentionally stymied, not well known, and underpaid by the industry. In the following decade, as the conservative and old-fashioned Eisenhower age gave way to the turbulent 1960s, fashion changed. For the country's younger generation of designers, the next decade would take fashion to another splashy Pop Art-infused plane.

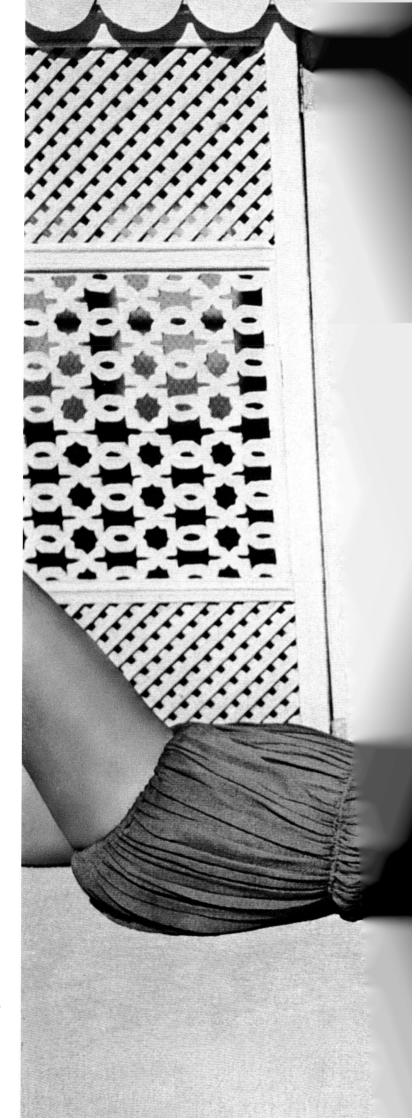

Claire McCardell, 1950
McCardell's sportswear, such as this bubble-shaped bathing suit, was highly influential and considered ahead of its time.

Maurice Rentner, ca.1954
Right   A Neiman Marcus advertisement
for Maurice Rentner. In 1959, he merged
with his sister Anna Miller's firm whose
in-house designer was Bill Blass.

Ben Zuckerman, 1953
Opposite   Romanian-born Zuckerman
was known for his elegant coats and suits.
Here Horst captures his taupe wool and
velvet suit for *Vogue*.

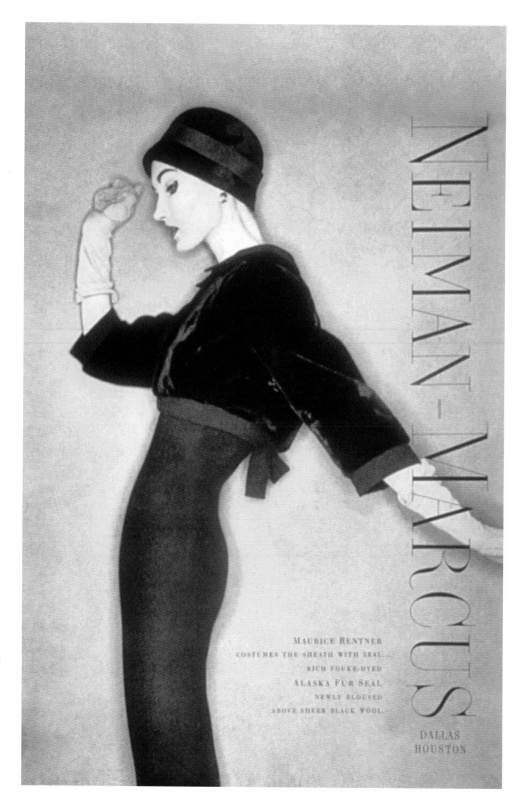

MAURICE RENTNER
COSTUMES THE SHEATH WITH SEAL...
RICH FOUKE-DYED
ALASKA FUR SEAL,
NEWLY BLOUSED
ABOVE SHEER BLACK WOOL

DALLAS
HOUSTON

Adele Simpson, 1953
Above   Spanish matador Dominguín
was an internationally known celebrity
during the 1950s. He was the inspiration
for Ernest Hemingway's *A Dangerous
Summer* and possibly for Simpson, whose
short bolero jacket over a brown velvet
wool dress is featured here with a fur
hat by Superb.

Traina-Norell, 1951
Opposite   Louise Dahl-Wolfe captures
a model in Traina-Norell's New Look
inspired ensemble for *Harper's Bazaar*.

Charles James, 1950
Above *Life* magazine captures a model in a James ensemble at a New York fashion show.

James Galanos, 1956
Opposite Philadelphia-born Galanos worked as a young man for Jean Louis at Columbia Pictures before studying in Paris with couturier Robert Piguet. Here is Galanos's brown speckled silk evening dress shot by Richard Rutledge for *Vogue*.

Pauline Trigère, 1947
Previous page, left Paris-born Trigère worked for Martial et Armand couture house before arriving in the United States in 1937. She worked for Ben Gershel, Travis Banton, and Hattie Carnegie before opening her own house in 1942. Here, John Rawlings captures Trigère's elegant silver evening dress.

Handmacher, 1949
Previous page, right Mary Jane Russell dons Handmacher's elegant suit for Louise Dahl-Wolfe for *Harper's Bazaar*.

Ceil Chapman, 1952

Above Debutantes like Beatrice Wagstaff, shot by Horst for *Vogue*, coveted Chapman's ball gowns and evening clothes throughout the 1950s.

Hattie Carnegie, 1952

Opposite Mrs. Winston F. C. Guest (a.k.a. C. Z.) was one of America's foremost fashion icons and was feted as "the greatest beauty of her time" by *Time* magazine in 1962. Guest wears a Carnegie gown of white piqué tied back with three pink satin bows.

Lord & Taylor, ca. 1950

Below Samuel Lord and George Washington Taylor founded the New York department store Lord & Taylor in 1826. Lord & Taylor is well known for their signature newspaper advertising illustrations as well as their support of American designers.

Bonnie Cashin, 1952

Opposite Cashin was a costume designer for 20th Century Fox during most of the 1940s. Afterwards, she was a pioneer in designing versatile sportswear, including this reversible striped silk shantung shirt.

Luis Estévez, 1956

Left Cuban-born Estévez began designing under his own name in 1955. In 1956, after marrying Prince Rainier of Monaco, actress Grace Kelly chose Estévez's gown of imported white Chantilly lace for her first royal portrait by artist Ralph Cowan.

Elizabeth Arden, 1951

Opposite Cosmetics pioneer Elizabeth Arden started an in-salon fashion boutique during World War II. Her designers included Charles James and, later, the young Oscar de la Renta. Here, Jacqueline Bouvier is seated with her sister, Caroline Lee Bouvier, in ball gowns from Arden shot by Cecil Beaton for *Vogue*.

Traina-Norell, 1957

Above A *Town & Country* story on "Dining in the Grand Manner," featuring Mr. and Mrs. F. Lee Zingale, of St. Louis, entertaining guests in the Plaza's Venetian suite. Mrs. Zingale wears a gold-sequin sheath, shadowed by a gold tulle stole.

Mainbocher, 1957

Opposite Mrs. Henry Ford II, the former Anne McDonnell, featured in *Vogue* wearing a dress by Mainbocher. Mainbocher was the establishment designer of choice for much of the 1950s with famous and wealthy clients across the country.

Mollie Parnis, 1953

Above   A model poses with a cigarette wearing a dress by Parnis and a gold and diamond necklace and bracelet by Van Cleef and Arpels.

Mainbocher, ca. 1960

Opposite   Mainbocher's career spanned four decades and two continents. Although a classicist at heart, he modernized his look during the 1960s. Here is his pink silk jacket worn with a simple black dress.

John-Frederics, 1952

John Piocelle and Frederic Hirst were first and foremost hat designers—although during the 1930s and 1940s they branched out to accessories, fragrances, and menswear. They designed hats for scores of Hollywood films from the 1930s through the 1950s, including the big straw hat with a green ribbon worn by Vivien Leigh in *Gone With the Wind* (1939). By the time Richard Avedon took this photo for *Harper's Bazaar*, Piocelle was operating under his Mr. John and John Juniors labels.

Jerry Parnis, 1952

Above Jerry Parnis competed with his designing sister and was known for his moderately priced dresses. Here Mary Jane Russell is captured in a modernist harem by Louise Dahl-Wolfe for *Harper's Bazaar.*

Mollie Parnis, 1957

Opposite Parnis's most famous client during the 1950s was First Lady Mamie Eisenhower. This orange dress is typical of the designer's feminine day wear. She later designed for First Ladies Pat Nixon and Betty Ford.

Irving Penn, 1947

"Twelve Beauties," New York. For more than six decades, Irving Penn's singular vision has graced the pages of *Vogue*. Often imitated but never rivaled is his iconic photograph of the era's most beautiful models wearing American fashion by Claire McCardell, Hattie Carnegie, Traina-Norell, Nettie Rosenstein, and Charles James.

Arnold Scaasi, 1957

Left An apprentice to Charles James and a freelance designer during the early 1950s, Scaasi launched his career in 1956 with a fashion show at the Plaza Hotel of twenty-three styles he created in his walk-up apartment. Buyers from three of America's most important stores—New York's Henri Bendel, Dallas's Neiman Marcus, and San Francisco's I. Magnin—bought every piece in the collection, launching Scaasi's five decade career.

Oleg Cassini, 1958

Opposite Cassini's ultra-feminine green dress accompanied by a hat by New York designer Sally Victor.

Irving Penn, 1950
Models Dorian Leigh and Evelyn Tripp,
together but alone, in Penn's memorable
photograph featuring Claire McCardell's
wool jersey dress and a jumper with leotard.

VOGUE

FEBRUARY 1

AMERICANA NUMBER

1955

The next successes in American fashion

How they look in a full-length mirror

GLAMOUR
for the girl with a job
48 ways to wear colour
advance retail trade edition
SPRING HAT NEWS
35 Cents
How to Have
a Colourful Personality

VOGUE
SUMMER PLANS:
The Black and White Idea
The Linen Life
Transparent Fashions
ADVANCE RETAIL TRADE EDITION
April 1, 1950
Price 50 Cents

BAZAAR
Harper's
Clothes for the
Air-Conditioned Climate
Clothes for
Summer Out-of-Doors
May 1954
60 cents

Mademoiselle
June 1959
50 cents
Special beauty issue
The star-spangled
beauty...
and how
to be one
Jason Robards, Jr...
and other stars answer:
What makes
the American girl
exciting?

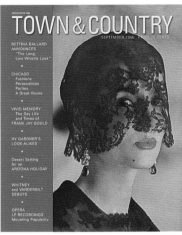

TOWN & COUNTRY
SEPTEMBER 1956. PRICE 75 CENTS
BETTINA BALLARD ANNOUNCES "The Long, Low Whistle Look"
CHICAGO Fashions Personalities Parties A Great House
VIVID MEMORY The Gay Life and Times of FRANK JAY GOULD
HY GARDNER'S LOOK-ALIKES
Desert Setting for an ARIZONA HOLIDAY
WHITNEY and VANDERBILT DEBUTS
OPERA LP RECORDINGS' Mounting Popularity

BAZAAR
SEPTEMBER 1955
60 CENTS

TIME
THE WEEKLY NEWSMAGAZINE
TWENTY CENTS
NEWS FROM PARIS & THE USA: A FULL FASHION REPORT
FASHION DESIGNER CLAIRE McCARDELL
VOL. LXV, NO. 18

GLAMOUR
December
Merry Christmas
for the girl with a job
25 cents
Gifts • Clothes • Parties

GLAMOUR
Young America Issue
Fall Fashion Forecast
July 1917
Price 25 Cents

BAZAAR
Harper's
Incorporating Junior Bazaar
The Winter Season
Lingerie
Christmas Gifts
November 1948
60 cents

Flair
NOVEMBER 1950 INTRODUCTORY ISSUE
COUNTRY LIVING

LIFE
DINA MERRILL: ACTRESS, SOCIALITE, SPRINGTIME MODEL
JANUARY 11, 1960   19 CENTS

TIME
THE WEEKLY NEWSMAGAZINE
LISA FONSSAGRIVES

MADEMOISELLE
The magazine for smart young women
November 1950
35 cents
Pre-holiday issue
Christmas gifts

PLAYBOY
ENTERTAINMENT FOR MEN
50c
FIRST TIME in any magazine FULL COLOR the famous MARILYN MONROE NUDE
VIP ON SEX

Mademoiselle
May 1959
50 cents
Your
freewheeling
summer
20 top trips
in the U.S.A.
Playclothes,
swimsuits,
American classics,
bonbon cottons

1961/1971

Space Age Youthquake

AMERICAN DESIGNERS
POP TO PROMINENCE

In 1961, soon after John and Jacqueline Kennedy moved into the White House, the Soviet Union managed to successfully put cosmonaut Yuri Gagarin into manned spaceflight. It was a tremendous coup for the Russians as Cold War rivalries and intrigues between the Soviet Union and the United States escalated. John Glenn's orbit in February 1962 evened the score, but the race to the moon continued until Neil Armstrong's first moonwalk in 1969. Back on planet earth, the young and attractive First Family epitomized the country's changing dynamics and demographics. The baby boom was palpable as Kennedy announced in his inaugural address, "A torch has passed to a new generation."

Jacqueline Bouvier, winner of *Vogue*'s coveted Prix de Paris award as a college student in 1951, was already a familiar face to followers of fashionable America, and her appearance in magazines and newspapers would only increase after her marriage to Ambassador Joseph P. Kennedy's son in 1953 in Newport, Rhode Island. By 1959, through her active presence on her husband's campaign, Jacqueline Kennedy was already known for her elegant and modern style—in stark contrast to the staid propriety of the Eisenhower years. She was no feminist revolutionary, claiming in frequent interviews that her priorities were, first, as a wife and mother. What was so extraordinary about the young First Lady was that though she embraced the traditional role of women, she was able to communicate her own youthful fashion sensibility while maintaining the decorum her role required. This exacting attitude pervaded all her activities, from the planning of state dinners to her acclaimed historical restoration of the White House.

Jacqueline Kennedy's look was pared down and unadorned—save for simple decorative flourishes or the occassional single piece of jewelry. She favored bright pastel shades in her day clothes and dramatic yet simple evening wear. In her private life, Mrs. Kennedy was partial to the elegant and modern work of Paris couturier Hubert de Givenchy. The use of American fashion designers had been almost mandatory for every First Lady since Eleanor Roosevelt. Oleg Cassini created most of Mrs. Kennedy's White House wardrobe, though prominent Americans such as Gustave Tassell, Roy Halston, Herbert Sondheim, Joan Morse, Norman Norell, and Donald Brooks also contributed to her look. She influenced American

Bill Blass, 1967
Opposite Blass had taken over Maurice Rentner's business in his own name the year Richard Avedon captured Verushka in one of his evening mini-dresses. Blass also began designing menswear and featured his own image in advertising with taglines such as "Who needs Paris when you can steal from yourself."

Ben Reig/Adolfo, 1964
Previous pages Location photography became the rage during the 1960s. Here, a model stands on Cornwallis Island at the Arctic Circle, wearing Reig's winter-white silk faille evening cape with mink-edged hood, a matching helmet by Adolfo, and silver sequined gloves.

fashion simply because she looked so good in whatever she wore. The pink embroidered Cassini gown Kennedy selected for a dinner hosted by President Charles de Gaulle at the palace of Versailles served as a turning point in our country's fashion history. As American fashion's ambassador, Jacqueline Kennedy, an American beauty of French descent, spoke the foreign language beautifully, charming the entire world in her elegant American gown and poised demeanor.

While American designers had made great strides during the 1950s, most of the emerging talents from that decade remained largely anonymous. Eleanor Lambert believed that America's fashion designers would be better served if they came together as a group with a common purpose. Lambert's urgings led to the founding of the Council of Fashion Designers of America (CFDA) in 1962. Founding members, led by first president Sydney Wragge, included Bill Blass, Donald Brooks, Luis Estévez, Rudi Gernreich, Jean Louis, Norman Norell, Gustave Tassell, Pauline Trigère, Ferdinando Sarmi, Arnold Scaasi, and Ben Zuckerman. The Coty Awards, which reached their height during World War II, continued to be one of the most prestigious marks of achievement during the next two decades. Neiman Marcus's Award for Distinguished Service in the Field of Fashion, launched in 1938, also recognized achievement in the industry.

After *Vogue* lured Diana Vreeland from *Harper's Bazaar* in 1962, fashion in America would be shaken up in new ways. Youth was the currency of the time, and Vreeland quickly shifted the magazine—and fashion—toward this new realm. Her peripatetic and larger-than-life imagination inspired designers, editors, and photographers to reinvent fashion in ways that reflected the changing world—transforming her into a fashion legend of historic importance. She and her editors championed American fashion on the same level that they championed Yves Saint Laurent in Paris or Mary Quant in London. Alexander Liberman, who helped bring Vreeland to *Vogue*, collaborated with her to capitalize on the talents of photographers such as Irving Penn, Richard Avedon, Henry Clarke, and Bert Stern in remaking the magazine. The widening availability of jet travel allowed for an ever increasing use of exotic location photography. Vreeland sent her fashion editors, such as Babs Simpson, Grace Mirabella, Susan Train, and Polly Mellen (frequently with photographer Henry Clarke in tow accompanied by top models such as Marisa Berenson and Veruschka), to remote locations around the world. These trips culminated in *Vogue*'s annual Christmas issue—evidence that the fashion magazine had become not only a source of information but entertainment as well. Other influential fashion publications such as *Women's Wear Daily* and *The New York Times'* "Fashion of the Times," as well as editors and publishers including Eugenia Sheppard, Carrie Donovan, and John Fairchild also chronicled the rise of American fashion during the decade.

Vreeland, along with other magazine and newspaper editors, recognized an explosion of new fashion sources, including hip boutiques like Paraphernalia and Serendipity, that were popping up all over the country,

tracking down fads and novelties not only in New York and California but also in Paris, London, and Milan. While Norman Norell, Pauline Trigère, and Mainbocher continued to lead the Establishment, younger designers, including Geoffrey Beene, Bill Blass, Donald Brooks, Luis Estévez, Oscar de la Renta, and Arnold Scaasi, came to the forefront during this innovative and convention-defying epoch.

The "youthquake" cocktail of American fashion during the period took inspiration from the rapidly changing landscape of Pop and Op Art, ethnic clothing, the proliferation of synthetic fabrics, hippie, or bohemian chic, rock music, and avant-garde and experimental creative outpourings stemming from such disparate sources as Andy Warhol's Factory and the Woodstock Music Festival. Tie-dyed, batik fabrics, and ethnographic and contemporary art-inspired textiles were all blended into the hybrid fashion look of the 1960s. Socially, as women tore off their bras and took birth control pills, they found fashion freedom in blue jeans, vintage clothing, and wares from seemingly unfashionable sources such as military surplus stores.

While the editorial choices of Vreeland and other influential fashion tastemakers captured the zeitgeist for most of the 1960s, the growing unrest kindled by the civil rights movement and the increasingly unpopular war in Vietnam was taking its toll. Times moved ahead, but Vreeland continued on in her fantasies ignoring the grimmer truths of the Nixon era. By the beginning of the 1970s, Vreeland's extravagance had disgruntled many fashion advertisers. Grace Mirabella would replace her in 1971, with Vreeland moving her spectacular and theatrical style to the Metropolitan Museum of Art's Costume Institute, where she would mount a series of groundbreaking fashion exhibitions in the decade to come.

Another fashion development of the 1960s was the emergence of designer menswear, a new type of men's clothing designed outside of traditional tailoring. Men's clothes became more fanciful, with early designers finding inspiration in the looks of the street as well as in fashion capitals such as Paris, London, and Milan. Notably, Ralph Lauren, who began designing neckties in the late 1960s, won the first Coty Award for menswear in 1970.

Other prominent American fashion designers of the period included Larry Aldrich, Anne Fogarty, Stephen Burrows, Bonnie Cashin, Anne Klein, Betsey Johnson, Stan Herman, Giorgio Sant'Angelo, and Lilly Pulitzer. Hats became unfashionable, with Halston and Adolfo abandoning their millinery businesses and turning to clothing. Veteran Mollie Parnis continued to design her popular looks with Pop-inspired flavor as her loyal clients, including First Ladies Lady Bird Johnson and Pat Nixon, embraced her mainstream fashion. Jean Louis and James Galanos, as well as bathing-suit designer Tom Brigance, continued to represent the California contingent of American fashion as the nation moved toward the pivotal 1970s.

Gustave Tassell, 1962

Right First Lady Jacqueline Kennedy wears Tassell's pale yellow silk dress on her official visit to Jaipur, India, accompanied by U.S. ambassador and economist John Kenneth Galbraith.

Oleg Cassini, 1961

Opposite Norman Norell and Sarmi competed with Cassini for the opportunity to design Jacqueline Kennedy's official wardrobe. Mrs. Kennedy preferred simple, unadorned clothing during the era and was said to have preferred solid bright colors—as did Queen Elizabeth and the Queen Mother—for public appearances and photographic opportunities. Here, Frank Sinatra escorts Kennedy to the Inaugural Ball, where she wore Cassini's simple but elegant white satin gown. Cassini's fashion collaboration with the First Lady made him a household name across the country.

Donald Brooks, ca. 1970

Below   Donald Brooks also designed costumes for the theater, television, and film, including *Star!* (1968) with Julie Andrews. Here, a model poses in Donald Brooks's Op Art-inspired geometric-patterned dress.

Oscar de la Renta, 1969

Opposite   Princess Elizabeth of Toro models a dress at de la Renta's first collection presented in his showroom.

Lilly Pulitzer, 1964

Following pages   When Pulitzer's boarding school classmate Jacqueline Kennedy appeared in *Life* magazine in one of her bright-colored shifts, what had been a high-society exclusive to the Hamptons or Palm Beach became a national rage. In this image, Slim Aarons captures a group of Palm Beach ladies dressed in Pulitzer.

Luis Estévez, 1964

Below American fashion designers began touring the country with their collections during the 1960s. Here, Estévez, (left) is seen with *Hair* producer Michael Butler and Butler's wife Lois on their polo grounds. Mrs. Butler wears Estévez's chiffon and wool plaid hostess dress in camel and pale blue.

Jo Copeland, 1965

Opposite Copeland designed day and evening wear for Patullo from the 1940s until the 1970s. Actors Art Carney, Walter Matthau, and director Mike Nichols lie at the feet of Verushka, who is wearing Copeland's bias-cut dress in light wool jersey.

Halston, 1969

Below Diana Vreeland frequently sent American photographer Henry Clarke abroad for the special Christmas issues of *Vogue* during the 1960s. This shoot, in Iran, featured Marisa Berenson in Halston's tie-dyed velvet robe and puffy blue jersey pants by Sibley Coffee.

Oscar de la Renta, 1966

Opposite The Dominican-born de la Renta was a protégé of the influential Baron Nicolas de Gunzberg, who served as editor of both *Vogue* and *Harper's Bazaar* and as editor-in-chief of *Town and Country*. First a designer for Elizabeth Arden, replacing Sarmi, de la Renta was on his own by the time Marisa Berenson donned his hippie chic caftan for *Vogue*.

Bill Blass, 1965

Below A black-and-white giraffe-print tunic and pant ensemble modeled by Gloria Vanderbilt for Francesco Scavullo.

Pauline Trigère, 1964

Opposite *Vogue* sent Henry Clarke to Sicily to photograph this dramatic ensemble by Trigère, whose career spanned more than 50 years.

Giorgio Sant'Angelo, ca. 1971

Below Diana Vreeland was an early advocate of the Florence-born Sant'Angelo, using him as a stylist for *Vogue* before he opened his own business in California in 1966. Betsey Pickering Theodoracopulos wears his brocaded leotard with chiffon sleeves and tights.

Willi Smith, 1972

Opposite Smith came out with his own label in 1976 after freelancing for a firm called Digits. Actress Pamela Hensley wears Smith's halter top and pants in a record shop.

Arnold Scaasi, 1967

Above Scaasi was known for his craftsmanship and willingness to create far-out
silhouettes with boldly-patterned fabrics.
Two models pose in Scaasi's Pop Art–
inspired multicolored striped dresses.

Michael Mott–Paraphernalia, 1969

Opposite Boutiques were all the rage
during the 1960s—Paraphernalia was the
most famous of them. It opened in 1965
and soon had branches across the country.
Here, a model wears Mott's black velour
polo-shirt minidress with a double-
wrapped white leather belt.

Stan Herman, 1968

Above The American West-inspired Herman, seen here, with a model wearing his signature 1960s look.

Donald Brooks, 1971

Opposite This African-inspired brown, black, and white cotton print jacket and ankle-length skirt is a bold example of Brooks's bohemian-chic look of the late 1960s and early 1970s.

Molly Parnis, 1969

Below Penelope Tree poses for a *Vogue* photo shoot in Kashmir. She wears one of Parnis's creations emblematic of the bright palette of the 1960s.

Mary McFadden, 1969

Opposite Mary McFadden at her home outside Johannesburg wearing a Basutoland hat and a coolie dress made from an East African textile. McFadden's designs echo her early exotic and eclectic inspirations and influences.

VOGUE

75¢
MAY

THIS SUMMER'S FASHION
75 WONDERFUL NEW WAYS TO LOOK

THIS SUMMER'S BEAUTY
THE NEW SKIN IDE

  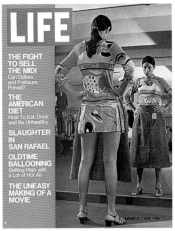 

 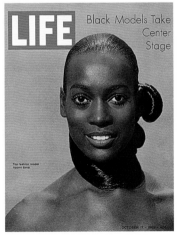  

1972/1980

American Fashion Arrives

BEIGE CHIC
TO DISCO INFERNO

Cathy Hardwick, 1975
Opposite Hardwick's fashion mantra requires simplicity of form. Here, simple yet sexy, off-the-shoulder one-piece pantsuits.

Fernando Sánchez, ca. 1975
Previous pages Spanish-born Sánchez studied fashion in Paris with his friend Yves Saint Laurent. He started his own business in New York in 1974 and was influential in popularizing elegant loungewear. Here, a model lounges with a beau in a very 1970s interior, wearing Sánchez's red cotton caftan dress.

The fantasy- and Pop Art–inspired fashions of the 1960s quickly gave way to a more grounded reality—at least during the early years of the 1970s. Emotionally, Americans were exhausted and disillusioned—war weary from Vietnam, increasingly concerned about the environment, feeling the heat of double-digit inflation, and distrustful of government. Issues first posed in the 1960s, such as civil rights, feminism, the environment, gay rights, drug usage, and birth control, entered into mainstream culture with increasing relevance. For the first time, America realized its dependence on energy sources in the Middle East, as the Arab oil embargo in 1973 direly affected the American economy. With gas lines, spiraling inflation, Watergate, and New York City on the verge of bankruptcy in 1975, there were few bright spots as Gerald Ford led America in its 1976 bicentennial celebration. The cardigan-sweater-wearing Sunday school teacher President Jimmy Carter lectured the nation on energy conservation as he fretted about the American hostages in Iran.

Ever since Dorothy Shaver began to promote American designers during the early 1930s, American fashion, with the exception of the war years, had continued to play second fiddle to the French. The 1960s had seen international fashion influences spread to London, Milan, and Tokyo. In November 1973, Eleanor Lambert produced a benefit fashion show at the palace of Versailles outside Paris, featuring fashion from ten French and American designers. Yves Saint Laurent, Christian Dior, Hubert de Givenchy, Emanuel Ungaro, and Pierre Cardin represented the French; Bill Blass, Oscar de la Renta, Anne Klein, Stephen Burrows, and Halston represented America. The festivities, produced and designed by fashion illustrator Joe Eula, included performances by Josephine Baker and Liza Minnelli—an extravaganza that presaged the seasonal multi-million-dollar runway spectacles and events that take place regularly in today's world fashion capitals. While critics felt that James Galanos and Geoffrey Beene were considerable omissions, Versailles was a turning point, and by the next decade American fashion was recognized and available throughout the world. With their well-received presentations seen in such a high-style, old-world setting, American designers upstaged their rivals in the world capital of fashion.

Fashion magazines were changing as well. Nancy White, who was editor of *Harper's Bazaar* through the 1960s, was briefly replaced by Jim Brady before *Town & Country's* editor Anthony Mazzola took over in 1972. Mazzola, an art director, brought over former *Vogue* editor Carrie Donovan, as well as a host of the era's top photographers, including Bill King, Rico Pullman, Francesco Scavullo, and Albert Watson. Grace Mirabella, aided and abetted by influential Condé Nast editorial director Alexander Liberman, quickly moved *Vogue* from the camp fantasies of the Vreeland years to a more realistic and *haut bourgeois* plain. Falling advertising revenues led publishers and editors to attract readers by offering real fashion for real people. *Vogue,* with its army of top photographers like Richard Avedon, Deborah Turbeville, Irving Penn, Arthur Elgort, and Helmut Newton and its fashion message for the modern American woman, climbed to more than a million subscribers during the 1970s. Featuring notable personalities and addressing the eras controversial social issues and current trends became a new editorial approach for magazines. Hence, in fashion, women were offered a menu of personal preferences, rather than fashion imposed from on high. Even hemlines, the classic mode indicator, were offered at optional levels ranging from miniskirts to midis and finally maxis. Fashion designers were quick to embrace the pulse of the 1970s as American women increasingly balanced career and family. Fashion of the period reflected these demands: work-appropriate pantsuits, blazers, and wrap dresses, allowing women to transition easily from day to night and from the office to a night on the town.

The evolving American lifestyle during the 1970s, of "having it all," required extra stamina; American men and women embraced sport and exercise as essential components of 1970s modern lifestyle. The democratization of the workplace, sexual politics, racial equality, and new focuses on health and diet all combined to transform American society, and the fashions that mirrored it, dramatically. Clothing became more comfortable; hairstyles and accessories more naturalistic and minimalist. How American designers interpreted 1970s modes of dress ranged from a sexy, casual femininity to a more masculine-tinged wardrobe of business suits and dresses.

Across the country, both women and men favored longer hair and more casual looks—sports clothes, sneakers, and blue jeans were worn by a wider range of people. When Ralph Lauren designed the men's costumes for the 1974 film *The Great Gatsby,* he inspired a nostalgia for sports clothes of the 1920s and 1930s. Along with the designs of Perry Ellis and others, these fashions led to a preppy look that would inform developments in men's and women's clothing during the 1980s. Diane Keaton's costumes in Woody Allen's *Annie Hall* (1977) captured the trend of a more masculine style of clothing for women. Designer clothes for men also became more prevalent during the era, with many of America's leading talents launching lines for men. Designers became celebrities in their own right; Bill Blass and Calvin Klein posed for editorial spreads in magazines and came to rely on slickly produced advertising to get their individual fashion messages across. Visible designer logos, labels, and brand icons were used with increasing frequency on clothing. Licensing flourished as designers lent their names to a cornucopia of products and accessories, beginning with fragrances,

sunglasses, purses, and scarves, and moving on to cars, airplanes, and myriad other products.

By the decade's end, the free, wearable, and empowering styles of the '70s gradually gave way as new influences in popular music and the arts reflected a change in American values and social conventions. Glamour Rock and Punk rock emerged as a new force in music, and finally there was disco. Together, these musical reactions to the folk and soft rock music that dominated most of the 1970s were nothing short of a cultural revolution. Mainstream stars of entertainment and fashion embraced the disco revolution—themselves becoming stars of nightlife as the music once heard only in black and gay clubs rose in currency, thanks to films like *Saturday Night Fever* (1977) and nightclubs like the much-imitated, but never rivaled, Studio 54.

Most of the designers of the decade focused on ready-to-wear though Scaasi, Galanos, and Halston continued to supply couture for their elite buyers. Masters from the past decade such as Geoffrey Beene, Bill Blass, Donald Brooks, Rudi Gernreich, Luis Estévez, Oscar de la Renta, and Pauline Trigère were joined by a host of talented new designers such as John Anthony, Stephen Burrows, Liz Claiborne, Perry Ellis, Norma Kamali, Cathy Hardwick, Anne Klein, Calvin Klein, Mary McFadden, Giorgio Sant'Angelo, and Diane von Furstenberg. And while each made signature contributions to American fashion in the 1970s, it was Roy Halston who most personified the decade. Halston's casually modern and free-flowing clothing, frequently accessorized by Elsa Peretti's nature-inspired jewelry and accessories, captured the taste of the country's most fashionable and was widely emulated. Halston became synonymous with 1970s style, with paparazzi capturing him and his famous friends like Liza Minnelli and Andy Warhol. Halston's lifestyle had as much to do with his popularity as his fashion itself. The decade also saw the emergence of several African-American designers, including Stephen Burrows, as well as African-American models such as Beverly Johnson, Norma Jean Darden, Alva Chinn, and Pat Cleveland. They broke racial boundaries on magazine covers and in fashion shows as well as in advertising. But the model of the decade was Lauren Hutton. Her imperfect beauty and casual elegance gave America identity, as expressed in Helen Reddy's feminist anthem, "I Am Woman" (1972).

The interregnum presidency of Gerald Ford, with maverick First Lady Betty Ford's candor concerning her bouts with breast cancer and substance abuse, revealed just how far the American woman had come. The arrival of Jimmy Carter, despite his plain-speaking and down-home charm, did little to lift Americans' spirits as they were urged to conserve energy. Finally, the hostage crisis after the fall from power of the Shah of Iran further crippled America's national identity. Many Americans instead chose to dance the night away, hoping that the nightmares of the 1970s would all vanish before dawn. They awoke instead to the freeing of the hostages and the arrival of the Hollywood-produced couple Ronald and Nancy Reagan. Societal woes would be set aside as the allure of power and money took center stage in the 1980s.

Roy Halston and Geoffrey Beene, 1974

Below   Fluid elegance connects these Halston and Beene pantsuit designs for the 1970s woman on the go. Shot by Francesco Scavullo for *Vogue*.

Jackie Kennedy Onassis, ca. 1975

Opposite   During the 1970s, Onassis continued to influence fashion adopting the more natural style of the decade and joining the workforce as a book editor.

Mary McFadden, 1977

Following pages   McFadden was a special projects editor at *Vogue* during the 1960s before launching her own line in 1973. Her fashions were influenced by Asia and Africa, as well as the pleated silk clothing of the Venetian couturier Fortuny. Here, *Vogue* showed eight examples from McFadden's collection led by the designer herself.

Calvin Klein, 1979

Right   Bloomingdale's was the single largest advertiser in *The New York Times* during the 1970s—frequently featuring its in-store designer fashion boutiques and collections.

Stephen Burrows, 1979

Below   Henri Bendel was known for showcasing up-and-coming designers. This advertisement promoted Stephen Burrows who credits the store for his early success.

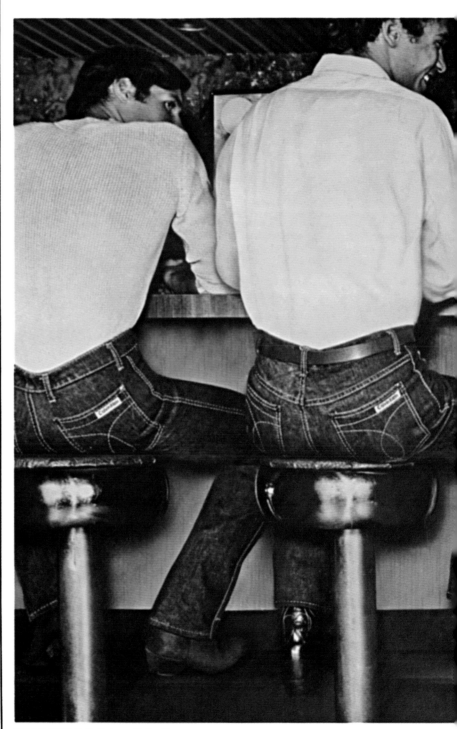

calvin klein '79... Inje

From our Calvin Klein Jean Collection,
the 5-pocket Western, 37.00
(her Calvin's, 35.00)

The Calvin Klein Shop for Men, Street Floor;
Designer Jeans, Escalator Level, New York.
Jenkintown and all fashion stores.

ous day after day
(didn't we tell you)

A first: Calvin Klein jeans for men. Some come with straight legs, some wi th narrow. Some come with a zipper up front, some with buttons. Some come with pockets, some without one in sight. They all come in deep indigo cotton denim, washed once for softness.

bloomingdale's
men's store

Roy Halston, 1972
Right More than any other designer of the 1970s, Halston lived the lifestyle his fashions evoked—the smoky and sexy lounge lizard out for a night on the town.

Joseph Abboud, ca. 1974
Opposite Abboud posed with models Appolonia (left) and Jerry Hall (right) in a photo shoot at the Hunting Inn in East Hampton for the famed retailer Louis of Boston.

Stephen Burrows, 1978
Right   Jerry Hall was one of America's top
supermodels during the 1970s and became
an international celebrity in her own right
through her tabloid romantic exploits with
Roxy Music's Bryan Ferry and the Rolling
Stone's Mick Jagger. At a fashion show,
she twirls in Burrows's turquoise satin
tunic-and-pant ensemble—replete with
feather boa for a quintessential disco look.

Diane von Furstenberg, 1972
Opposite   Von Furstenberg models her
signature wrap dress, an innovative
design that came to symbolize the era's
new freedom and ease.

Stephen Burrows, 1976

Above Stephen Burrows's color-blocked gowns were a definitive break from the 1960s mod mood. His characteristic dresses with signature lettuce edges were sexy, laid-back, and feminine—evoking the spirit of the freer 1970s woman.

Bill Blass, 1976

Opposite A model wears Blass's long dark overcoat with black mink lining and silk "rainshell," paired with jersey straight-leg pants in a photo for *Vogue*.

Rudi Gernreich, 1975

Following pages Austrian-born and notorious inventor of the *monokini*, Gernreich pushed the fashion envelope with his futuristic designs. *Vogue* featured his controversial thong bathing suits, captured by Helmut Netwon.

Alexander Julian, 1977

Right   Julian, an American pioneer in men's fashion, created his own exclusive fabrics.

Liz Claiborne, 1975

Below   Claiborne started in the 1950s as an illustrator for Tina Leser and subsequently for Omar Kiam at Ben Reig. During the 1960s and early 1970s, she designed for a line called Youth Guild before setting out on her own in 1976. Below, a model poses in a cream blouse and shiny black skirt typical of Claiborne's casual style.

Calvin Klein, 1979

Opposite   Calvin Klein struck out on his own in 1968 and became one of the most influential designers for the next several decades, known as much for his glamorous lifestyle as for his modernist- and minimalist-inspired clothes. Here, Roxanne Lowit captures the designer.

Ralph Lauren, 1979

Following pages   Inspired by everything from film to the American West, Lauren, seen here, gave traditional country clothing an elegant and more formal appearance in both his day and evening collections.

Bergdorf Goodman, ca. 1975

Below For over over a century, Bergdorf Goodman has served New York City women as the go-to destination for high-style fashion. In 1914, Goodman became the first couturier to introduce ready-to-wear. In this photograph set in its Art Deco-style store, Andrew Goodman, president and chairman of Bergdorf Goodman, views selections from the store's collections.

Diane von Furstenberg, ca. 1975

Opposite Cheryl Tiegs models von Furstenberg's wrap two-piece pantsuit. Her signature wrap dresses and suits were among the most popular fashion ensembles of the era.

Giorgio Sant'Angelo, 1977

Below   Christie Brinkley captured by Arthur Elgort in Sant'Angelo's custom string tied bikini for *Vogue*.

Calvin Klein, 1976

Opposite   Klein understood that dressing the woman of the 1970s was more about attitude than any particular fashion statement. His novel merchandising made him one of America's most influential designers for decades. Here, Patti Hansen models Klein's minimalist swimsuit.

Halston, 1979

Following pages   A regular at Studio 54, Halston became synonymous with New York City's thriving nightlife, immortalized in Sister Sledge's disco anthem "He's the Greatest Dancer"—"Halston, Gucci, Fiorucci." In this portrait by Roxanne Lowit, Halston reviews design sketches in his studio.

Luis Estévez, 1970

Below   Estévez moved to Southern California in 1968. During the 1970s and 1980s, he was a favorite of Hollywood's entertainment stars and social set and designed gowns for Betty Ford and Nancy Reagan during their years in the White House. When he started a swimwear line in 1970, this white Lycra maillot with a tied, grommeted bust was a bestseller.

Carolina Herrera, ca. 1970

Opposite   An international social figure in the 1970s, Herrera's elegant and modern personal style would inform her fashion business when she opened in the early 1980s.

Studio 54, 1978

Following pages   The ultimate 1970s discotheque, where the rich and famous mingled with the merely young and beautiful. Halston, Bianca Jagger, Liza Minnelli, and Andy Warhol air-kiss and chit-chat for the paparazzi on New Year's Eve.

201

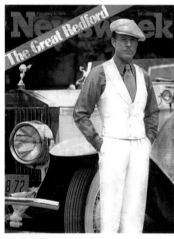

1981/1999

Brand Name Stars

DYNASTY GLAMOUR
TO STREET-SMART GRUNGE

Always a mirror of its times, fashion—particularly American fashion—became a dominant force in the 1980s. Supersonic jet travel, the launch of CNN in 1980, and the sheer volume of cable TV selections—MTV-style entertainment, home shopping channels, and fashion-based news networks pioneered by CNN's Elsa Klensch—precipitated the tremendous world reach of American fashion, as many designers were transformed into global brands.

The Reagan years were marked by a frenzied celebration of luxury and ostentation thanks in part to the fashion-loving First Lady, Nancy Reagan. Billionaires replaced millionaires and were chronicled in books like Tom Wolfe's *The Bonfire of the Vanities* and films like Oliver Stone's *Wall Street*, both of which appeared in 1987. The zeitgeist of the era was reflected in a range of other areas of popular culture: TV series like *Dynasty* and *Dallas*; the rise of black-tie charity balls and benefits such as the Metropolitan Museum of Art's annual "Party of the Year" for its Costume Institute; the annual Academy Awards ceremony broadcast to an increasingly global audience and the meteoric rise of celebrities from Madonna to Michael Jackson to talk-show hosts and lifestyle gurus like Oprah Winfrey and Martha Stewart.

Thanks to Mrs. Reagan's penchant for the luxurious work of couturier James Galanos and designers Bill Blass, Adolfo, Geoffrey Beene, and Oscar de la Renta, these fashion veterans saw increased media exposure. Along with other designers of evening wear, their upscale ready-to-wear lines were featured in specialty stores as women sought out lavish ball gowns for the opulent parties, society weddings, and benefit balls that took place under the Reagan as well as the first George Bush presidencies. It was during these years that fashion shows became entertainment events in themselves. In 1992, the Council of Fashion Designers of America, under the leadership of President Stan Herman, created New York Fashion Week. For the first time, there was a central location for fashion editors and buyers to view the collections, usually at the enormous temporary building erected in the city's Bryant Park. These twice-annual events have become cornerstones in the international fashion calendar, and while some designers stage events around the city during the collections, they stage them taking full advantage of the international exposure that Fashion Week affords.

From the late 1970s through the early 1990s, major department stores began promoting designers extravagantly, featuring in-store individual designer boutiques and sophisticated advertising campaigns in print and on television. Bloomingdale's CEO Marvin Traub, along with advertising aficionados Gordon Cooke and John Jay and fashion-buying legend Kal Ruttenstein, brought their merchandizing savvy into play, furthering the profiles of competing fashion giants such as Calvin Klein and Ralph Lauren. Other influential merchants, such as Geraldine Stutz at Henri Bendel and Dawn Mello at Bergdorf Goodman, spotlighted American fashion design with increased frequency. The evolution of closely managed brand identities allowed designers to emerge as retailers themselves. In 1984, Lauren opened his first flagship store housed in the historic Gilded Age Rhinelander mansion on Manhattan's Upper East Side, expanding his retail activity into varied lines of merchandise ranging from men's and women's fashion, accessories, fragrances, and home furnishings. Like fellow designers Calvin Klein and Donna Karan, Tommy Hilfiger also became a brand throughout the world. Designers such as Isaac Mizrahi branched out to wider endeavors such as theater design, starring in his own cable-television program and designing a line of clothing and accessories for Target. Celebrities from the pop world also entered fashion design, such as Sean Combs and Gwen Stefani. The CFDA's annual fashion awards replaced the prestigious Coty Awards in 1984, marking a coming-of-age for the two-decades-old group. The new award, designed by contemporary artist Ernest Trova, underscored the CFDA's rising preeminence as the industry's leading organization.

Menswear came into its own as well-known womenswear designers expanded to design or license their names to everything from underwear to business suits. They were joined by designers who focused only on menswear such as Joseph Abboud, Jeffrey Banks, Jhane Barnes, John Bartlett, Alexander Julian, Bill Robinson, and Ronaldus Shamusk. While bejeweled evening gowns were all the rage at parties and power dressing was the office norm, unisex chain retailers Eddie Bauer, Esprit, The Gap, Levi Strauss, and Banana Republic provided more casual, everyday lines, becoming the retail giants they remain today. In 1988, Donna Karan extended her women's collection into a less expensive line, DKNY, for younger women. This trend was widely embraced by other fashion leaders.

Already an actress, Brooke Shields dominated magazine covers in the early 1980s, but as the decade progressed the phenomenon of the supermodel emerged. Dominated by "the Trinity"—Christy Turlington, Linda Evangelista, and Naomi Campbell—the presence of super models in both magazines and advertising campaigns led to a blurring of reportage and retail. Famous photographers like Bruce Weber, Annie Leibovitz, and Steven Meisel created sophisticated and costly ad campaigns featuring America's Cindy Crawford, Carolyn Murphy, and Stephanie Seymour.

Fashion coverage expanded exponentially: John Fairchild brought out *W* magazine celebrating fashion with a gossipy insouciance as a high-style, glossy sister to the influential trade newspaper *Women's Wear Daily*. After his death in 1987, Andy Warhol's *Interview* magazine morphed into a full-fledged fashion and entertainment magazine under editor-in-chief Ingrid Sischy. Foreign publishers launched American editions during the 1980s, most notably French publisher Hachette Filipacchi's American *Elle* led by creative director Gilles Bensimon. The arrival of British editors Anna Wintour to *Vogue* in 1988 and Liz Tilberis to *Harper's Bazaar* in 1992 ushered in new eras at those legendary publications. During the 1990s, Wintour's editorship of *Vogue* catapulted her to world recognition far outside the boundaries of magazines or fashion.

The New York Times covered American fashion with increasing regularity, thanks in part to legendary photographer Bill Cunningham, whose "On the Street" feature, as well as his fashion-show and society coverage, captured the era. Other leading fashion editors at *The Los Angeles Times* and *The Washington Post*, as well as Hebe Dorsey and later Suzy Menkes at *The International Herald Tribune*, championed American fashion designers, putting them on par with designers in Paris, London, and Milan. The "downtown" fashion and art scene was touted by *Soho Weekly News* fashion editor Annie Flanders, who went on to create the more mainstream hipster magazine *Details* before it was bought by Fairchild Publications and eventually morphed into a men's publication. *GQ*'s Art Cooper and *Esquire*'s Woody Hochswender were just two of the many celebrants of menswear.

The supermodel era dominated much of the 1980s. By the mid-1990s however, magazine covers more often featured actresses and pop stars, as individual designers forged endorsements and partnerships with these famous spokespeople. Television series such as *Sex in the City* expanded a perceived New York–based fashion sensibility to the country, and world. Likewise, the proliferation of e-commerce and merchant-based cable networks such as QVC and the Home Shopping Network created lucrative new venues for fashion marketing in America.

The darkest cloud, it seemed, was the AIDS epidemic that emerged in the early 1980s and affected every branch of the arts and entertainment into the 1990s. In a few years, hundreds of talents were lost. The pandemic's casualties included designers Willi Smith, Perry Ellis, Giorgio Sant'Angelo, Halston, Angel Estrada, Carmelo Pomodoro, the jewelry designer Tina Chow, and models Joe McDonald and Gia Carangi—to name only a small few—crippling the American fashion community.

Grunge emerged in the 1990s as the counterpoint to the excessive and ostentatious '80s. The Seattle-born mournful ennui of music by Kurt Cobain of Nirvana and Pearl Jam, replaced the peppy and playful New Wave and pop sounds of the 1980s. *Women's Wear Daily* nicknamed Marc Jacobs "the guru of grunge" after he presented a Seattle-inspired collection. The grunge aesthetic was in no small part the result of the sagging economy during the first Bush era, the dot-com crash as well as the first

Ralph Lauren, 1983
Opposite A group of models wear an all-American classic—the white Polo shirt.

Oscar de la Renta, 1987
Following pages During the 1980s, de la Renta's signature color was black, as evidenced in Arthur Elgort's portrait of the designer with ballet master Mikhail Baryshnikov and a bevy of de la Renta–gowned models.

Persian Gulf War. The economic recession dampened the optimistic mood that had helped fashion thrive in the 1980s. As a result, new talent was virtually nonexistent and established designers enjoyed less creative freedom. In a 1991 interview, Calvin Klein said: "There's a restructuring of priorities. It's less about flash…. People are becoming more real." As an antidote to grunge, Donna Karan, Geoffrey Beene, and Klein offered modernism and simplicity in black and neutral tones.

As a testament to how far American fashion had progressed, during the 1990s several of the CFDA's best-known designers took the helm at European fashion houses: Oscar de la Renta for Pierre Balmain, Tom Ford for Gucci, Michael Kors for Celine, John Bartlett for Byblos, and Marc Jacobs for Louis Vuitton later in the decade. Back at home, in 1998 the New York collections moved to the beginning of the international fashion season, ahead of London, Milan, and Paris.

The arrival of President Bill Clinton in office in 1993 with his controversial First Lady, Hillary, polarized the nation but also saw the American economy grow to new heights before scandals displaced the nation's attention at the end of the 1990s. Anna Wintour featured Mrs. Clinton dressed in Oscar de la Renta on the cover of the December 1998 issue of *Vogue* and as a result was widely credited with helping to reshape the First Lady's image as she moved out of the White House and was elected to the United States Senate in 2000.

At the turn of the millennium, an exhibition at the Metropolitan Museum of Art's Costume Institute of the White House–era clothes of Jacqueline Kennedy was a reminder of her profound influence on fashion during a pivotal period in America's history. First Lady Laura Bush, like her mother-in-law First Lady Barbara Bush, would come to rely on designers such as Scaasi and Oscar de la Renta. And with George W. Bush in the White House, extraordinary new challenges would be in store for America and the world soon after the start of the twenty-first century.

Louis Dell'Olio, 1992
Above Christy Turlington models
Dell'Olio's modernist white blouse and trim
black slacks. Donna Karan brought fellow
New Yorker Dell'Olio to codesign at Anne
Klein when Klein died in 1974.

Donna Karan, 1986
Opposite Rosemary McGrotha models
one of Donna Karan's early designs.

Geoffrey Beene, 1991
Below Gladys Perint Palmer, artist for many fashion designers, captures Beene's fluid elegance in her sketch of three Beene fashionistas.

Isabel Toledo, ca. 1990
Opposite Ruben Toledo's sketch of an Isabel Toledo design.

Zoran, ca. 1981
Left Yugoslavian-born Zoran, who trained as an architect, is a minimalist master. Patrick Demarchelier shot these Zoran models for *Vogue*.

Donna Karan, 1992
Following pages In the 1990s, Karan injected sex and power into women's wardrobes, from cashmere bodysuits to pin-striped power suits, fundamentally changing the way women dressed.

Saks Fifth Avenue, 1982

Below In 1924, Horace Saks and Bernard Gimbel opened Saks Fifth Avenue in New York City. Saks is among the major department stores responsible for American designers' nationwide success.

Perry Ellis, 1981

Left After designing clothing for various firms for almost two decades, Perry Ellis launched his own line in 1980 to immediate acclaim. Here, Ellis sits among models for his 1981 fashion show.

Above: the designers gather with models for a glittering finale. Left center: Geoffrey Beene with SFA Fashion Director Ellin Saltzman; Oscar de la Renta greeted by fans; Adolfo interviewed for Cable News Network.

Above: Merchandise Manager Alan Grosman with Mary McFadden; Arnold and Sheila Aronson.

Adri, ca. 1989
Right   Adri adored Claire McCardell
and emulated her dictum of "form
following function."

Richard Tyler, 1997
Opposite   Tyler started in menswear in
1987 and launched a women's collection
two years later that gained acclaim for
its impeccable tailoring, featured in this
image of Linda Evangelista shot by
Gilles Bensimon.

Isaac Mizrahi, 1991
Above Actress/model Joan Severance wears Mizrahi's "Totem Pole" dress in a photo by Steven White for *Harper's Bazaar.*

Bob Mackie, 1991
Opposite Mackie is most famous for his costume work. In this photo, a model shows off his theatrical style.

Anne Cole, 1986

Below   Anne Cole was born into the swimwear business—her father owned Cole of California, where she began to work in the 1950s. Matthew Rolston caught her popular and sexy bathing suit.

Stephen Sprouse, 1984

Opposite   Sprouse's punk-inspired day glo graffiti and camoflouge clothing brought the edgy downtown look into the mainstream of American fashion. He also designed costumes for the some of the top pop bands of the era including Blondie and Duran Duran. Actress Catherine Oxenberg wears Sprouse's tight graffiti pants and silk jersey t-shirt.

we believe in supreme lean. Uninterrupted from 13" ankle to one whittled waist. No confusion of contours. No distractions in sight — save a long, leggy unforgettable form. And this is what we like to see-under tunics, sweaters... or solo perhaps (how's that in the Hamptons?): jeans that never had to learn to be taut. They weren't made to be massive, they were bred to be born-again skin. Tight (read tourniquet) in cotton denim so durable it almost begs to be abused. So do so. Capriciously.

Calvin Klein's Capri Jeans, 4 to 12, 29.00. Third Floor. (Now all you need is a splas of his scent.)

bloomingdale's

1000 Third Avenue, New York. 355-900. Open late Monday and Thursday evenings.
Also available in Fresh Meadows, Garden City, White Plains Riverside Square-Bergen, Short Hills, Stamford, Tysons Corner and White Flint.

Adolfo, ca. 1981

Opposite   Fashion artist Antonio captures Adolfo's decadant gold gowns. Antonio first received acclaim at *Women's Wear Daily* when his Lilly Daché drawing appeared on the front page. He freelanced for *Vogue*, *Harper's Bazaar*, *Elle*, and *Interview* and worked closely with Charles James and Karl Lagerfeld, eventually metamorphosing and energizing fashion illustration.

Calvin Klein, 1981

Above   Calvin Klein started the designer jean craze in 1979, when young model Brooke Shields appeared in Klein's print and television advertisements claiming, "Nothing comes between me and my Calvins." Illustration by Antonio.

Jhane Barnes, 1985
Right   Menswear designer Barnes
was the first woman, and the youngest
designer, to win a Coty Award in 1980.
Here, a model dons one of Barnes's
signature tweed jackets.

James Galanos, 1981
Opposite   Nancy and Ronald Reagan
personified the 1980s taste for luxury and
glamour. She wore Galanos's white satin
sheath gown at her husband's Inaugural
Ball in 1981.

Norma Kamali, 1983

Below Diana Vreeland made news when she added Kamali's "parachute dress" to the permanent collection of the Metropolitan Museum of Art's Costume Institute. Kamali's body-hugging futurist red jumpsuit suggests the retro/future styles embraced by bands of the era such as the B52's and Talking Heads.

Diane von Furstenberg, ca. 1983

Opposite Von Furstenberg, captured here by Ara Gallant, was one of the dozens of American designers who licensed "designer jeans" and other casual clothes during the late 1970s and 1980s. They included society's Gloria Vanderbilt, as well as Jordache, Guess?, and Calvin Klein.

Adolfo, 1992

Following page, left Though Adolfo got his start designing hats for Emme, the Cuban-born designer began designing suits and gowns in 1963.

Bill Blass, 1994

Following page, right Known as much for his elegant evening wear as for his suits, Blass's exaggerated take on menswear features a striped-wool suit with a white necktie and an oversize coat.

Todd Oldham, 1995
Below　Amber Valletta, Linda Evangelista, and Cindy Crawford backstage at an Oldham fashion show in signature mosaic-print silk designs.

Isaac Mizrahi, 1994
Opposite　Christy Turlington, Naomi Campbell, and Gail Elliott walk the runway in a black-and-white grouping.

Isabel Toledo, 1989

Below A sculpted dress by Toledo,
photographed at the Metropolitan
Museum of Art.

Marc Jacobs, 1996

Opposite New York–born Jacobs,
photographed by Roxanne Lowit.

Yeohlee, 1994
A black double-faced strapless satin evening gown with a white underskirt.

Narciso Rodriguez, 1996
When John F. Kennedy Jr. wed Carolyn
Bessette in her custom-designed gown by
Rodriguez, the designer went from fashion
insider to international star. Photograph
by Denis Reggie.

MOSCOW: Can the Center Hold?

TIME
INTERNATIONAL

Super models
Beauty and the Bucks

AUSTRIA	S 30	FRANCE	F 17.00	IRELAND (incl. tax)	IR£1.50	NORWAY	Kr 17.00	SWITZERLAND	F 4.50
BELGIUM	F 100	GERMANY	DM 4.80	ISRAEL (incl. tax)	NS 5.90	POLAND	PLZ 18000.00	TURKEY (incl. tax)	TL 7000
CZECHOSLOVAKIA	CZC 35.00	GIBRALTAR	£1.50	ITALY	Lit 3500	PORTUGAL	Esc 375	UNITED KINGDOM	£1.40

ELLE

CASHMERES,
LEATHERS, FURS, FANTASIES,
ULTRABEAUTY AND
LUXE EXTRAS
TRES RICHE

DAVID BYRNE
ZEFFIRELLI
MICHEL GUERARD

OCTOBER 1986

Interview

Music
Cyndi Lauper

W

The Tight
of Fashion

Suzy Goes to the
Wedding of the Year

How Diets Hurt You

Fergie for Hire

Designer Diamonds

Plus: Dennis Quaid,
Donna Karan and the
Last of the Great Walkers

Red-Hot Fall Clothes

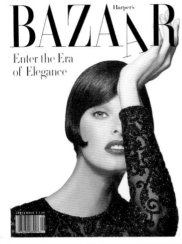

Harper's
BAZAAR

Enter the Era
of Elegance

W

Nicole Kidman

Oh,
Boy!

RALPH LAUREN

VOGUE

JULY $3.00

FALL
SIGNALS

what looks
really count

skirts short or long
– the choice is yours!

coats fast starters

hair the cut that
works best

BEAUTY & THE BREAST
the new medical progress

LIFE

FROM
OUR FIRST
50 YEARS

BATHING
BEAUTIES

ALZHEIMER'S
HOW THREE
FAMILIES COPE
WITH THE
TRAGIC DISEASE

SPY CLAN
WHY THE
WALKERS
DID IT —
AND HOW
THEY GOT
CAUGHT

THE JUDDS
COUNTRY'S
ADORABLE
DUO

PAULINA SUITS UP
IN THE LATEST AND
TINIEST

VOGUE

DECEMBER $3.00

STAR
TURNS:
LOOKS THAT
MAKE THE SEASON

KNOCKOUT
GLAMOUR:
GOLD, DIAMONDS,
WINTER WHITE

DRESS
FOR LESS:
SILVER AND
SEQUINS

GREAT
ESCAPE:
BEST RESORT BUYS

SPECIAL HOLIDAY ISSUE

VOGUE

DEC. $3.00

STANDOUTS

glorious
fashion!
new color excitement
freer, barer, softer looks

young hollywood
after the brat pack

GLORIOUS BROOKE:
BEAUTY/FITNESS
SPECIAL

Harper's
BAZAAR

Seasonless
Fashion:
The New Way
to Dress
Sexy Suits, Spring
Leathers, Delicate
Tops, Sharp Shoes

The Next Black Dress

Couture Quake:
The Bad Boys Arrive

Rockin' Runways:
Why Patti, Stevie,
and Courtney Rule

24-Hour Beauty

Plus: Billy Crudup,
Gus Van Sant,
Michael Kors

Linda Evangelista
Wears Isaac Mizrahi

MARCH $3.00

GLAMOUR

NOV. $2.95

10 LBS
THINNER!
no diet
no exercise
no kidding

43 fast
facts on
MEN,
SEX,
LOVE

RETIN-A:
good news
and bad
from
women
using it

MAKEOVER
MARATHON
Have the
hair you always
wanted

FASHION
CONFIDENCE
a winner's guide

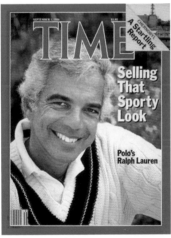

SEPTEMBER 1, 1986

A Startling
Report

TIME

Selling
That
Sporty
Look

Polo's
Ralph Lauren

Fashions of The Times

THE
SHAPES
OF SPRING

Mademoiselle

JANUARY 1986

intense!
the new eye...
soft & deep

56 terrific
today/tonight looks

real high finance:
drugs on wall street

"I've got a beauty secret"
(the sexy side of success)

THE FIGHT TO BE FRANCE'S FIRST LADY • THE JEWEL GARDEN • THE OPULENCE OF DAVID HICKS • THE TRUTH ABOUT CAPOTE

W

IT'S
PANTS!

Isaac Mizrahi

VANITY FAIR

MARCH 1992

$2.50

Goldie's Trunk Show
by Lynn Hirschberg

THE REAL PATRICIA BOWMAN
Dominick Dunne's Palm Beach Epilogue

THE FALL OF
THE HOUSE OF MAXWELL
by Edward Klein

MIKE TYSON'S TROUBLES
by Peter J. Boyer

2000...
Contemporary Directions

AMERICAN FASHION AT LARGE: GLOBAL IDENTITIES AND DISTINCTIVE VISIONS

American fashion in the twenty-first century is as diverse as culture itself. Gone are the days of fashion fascism or trendy fads—although each season has at least one "it" bag and shoe. Motifs of the new millennium are mosaic, and fashion both reflects and informs that reality. Rather than dictating a look, American designers offer unique visions of what contemporary clothing should be. From multiple spheres of aesthetics to collections for differing lifestyles, they interpret how contemporary men and women might dress.

Some of America's most famous and enduring designers, such as Oscar de la Renta and Ralph Lauren, remain active today with internationally regarded brand names and economically significant corporations. Ralph Lauren's vast empire is a public company traded on the New York Stock Exchange. Others have retired from fashion design, but their names live on. At Calvin Klein, creativity and newness flourish in the hands of Brazilian-born Francisco Costa (womenswear) and Italo Zucchelli (menswear). Donna Karan, who began opening eponymous retail stores only in 1999, now has stores throughout the country and the world—from London to Tokyo and Dubai.

The September 11 attack and subsequent military activities in the Middle East and around the world altered life in ways we cannot yet fully fathom. Nevertheless, days after the attack on the World Trade Center and the Pentagon, the American fashion world took action. Under the auspices of the CFDA and *Vogue* magazine, the community established Fashion for America, a campaign to restore consumer confidence that has since contributed more than $1.6 million to the Twin Towers Fund. And in 2005, the CFDA relaunched "Seventh on Sale" with a global online component, raising $1.7 million for HIV/AIDS organizations. The CFDA's Fashion Targets Breast Cancer has collectively raised more than $40 million for charities in Australia, Brazil, Canada, Cyprus, Greece, Ireland, Japan, Portugal, and Turkey. Many individual American designers also combine their fashion work with important philanthropic activities, such as Ralph Lauren's leadership in fighting breast cancer and Kenneth Cole's initiative in the HIV/AIDS pandemic, to name just two instances.

Ralph Lauren, 2007 *Opposite*

Zac Posen, 2004 *Previous pages*

In 1984, the CFDA Fashion Awards became the equivalent of the Academy Awards for the American fashion community. Recipients of CFDA awards represent a veritable pantheon of fashion talent both domestically and abroad. Besides its Designer of the Year awards in women's fashion, menswear, and accessories design, the CFDA also bestows its Swarovski's Perry Ellis Award for new talent, as well as a Lifetime Achievement Award and Special Tribute awards to notables throughout the fashion community. Winners have ranged from photographer Richard Avedon to designer Yves Saint Laurent. The Fashion Icon Award, bestowed on individuals whose personal style has had a profound influence on fashion, has been given to such luminaries as Audrey Hepburn, Lauren Bacall, Kate Moss, and Sarah Jessica Parker.

In addition to its prestigious annual CFDA Fashion Awards ceremony, the CFDA/*Vogue* Fashion Fund was established in 2003 to enable emerging talents to pursue their design careers. This initiative breathed new life into an industry under threat of becoming staid after the economic slump of the 1990s. Winners have so far included Proenza Schouler's Jack McCullough and Lazaro Hernandez (2004); Trovata's John Whitledge, Sam Shipley, Josia Lamberto-Egan, and Jeff Halmos (2005); and Doo-Ri Chung (2006). Runners-up are winners, too: to date, Habitual's Nicole and Michael Colovos and Cloak's Alexandre Plokhov (2004), Derek Lam and Thom Browne (2005), Rodarte's Laura and Kate Mulleavy and Thakoon's Thakoon Panichgul (2006).

Further confirming its importance in our culture, fashion coverage has expanded to horizons never imagined by designers of an earlier age. Virtually every medium now includes fashion reportage, from magazines and television to the Internet. American fashion designers not only dress celebrities for the red carpet but have also become celebrities themselves, with their designs and labels entering into the public consciousness, and magazines and Web sites quoting their opinions and documenting their lifestyles.

Thanks to the energy of champions of American fashion and the events and activities that are covered and supported worldwide, the designers of the new millennium are poised for uncharted horizons as American fashion enters its second century of singular creativity.

Thom Browne, 2004

Peter Som, 2006 *Below*

Ralph Rucci, 2006 *Opposite*

Oscar de la Renta, 2002 *Following pages*

Rick Owens, 2006 *Above*

Thakoon, 2007 *Opposite*

Carolina Herrera, 2003 *Previous pages*

Doo-Ri Chung, 2003 *Right*

Rodarte, 2007 *Below*

Calvin Klein, 2007 *Opposite*

Doo-Ri Chung, 2007 *Right*

J. Mendel, 2005 *Opposite*

VERY
BERGDORF

DOO.RI Meet the designer, here to present her Fall 2007 Collection, this Wednesday, 4–6pm. Collection available Wednesday and Thursday, 11am–6pm. Third Floor 212-753-7300

Anna Sui, 2006 *Below*
Derek Lam, 2006 *Opposite*

Trovata, 2005 *Above*

John Varvatos, 2007 *Left*

Tommy Hilfiger, 2003 *Following pages*

Diane von Furstenberg, 2006 *Below*

Marc Jacobs, 2004 *Opposite*

Ron Chereskin, 2006 *Right*

Maurice Malone, 2004 *Below*

John Bartlett, 2000 *Opposite*

BARNEYS
NEWYORK

Behnaz Sarafpour, 2004 *Below*
Narciso Rodriguez, 2007 *Opposite*

Donna Karan, 2003 *Below*

Rag & Bone, 2006 *Opposite*

Dennis Basso, 2005 *Right*
Nicole Miller, 2006 *Below*
Marc Jacobs, 2006 *Opposite*

Douglas Hannant, 2004 *Below*
Vera Wang, 2004 *Opposite*

Proenza Schouler, 2004 *Left*

Michael Kors, 2004 *Following pages*

293

HARPER'S

BAZAAR

FASHION IN AMERICA

BAZAAR KICKS OFF A SIX-CITY SERIES ON THE STATE OF STYLE

THE NAKED TRUTH

SARAH JESSICA PARKER HAS NOTHING TO HIDE

VANITY HAIR

WHY CAMERON, GWYNETH, AND WINONA CAN'T STOP CHANGING THEIR LOCKS

WOMEN IN POWER

5 LEADERS WHO ARE SHAPING YOUR WORLD

RED, WHITE, AND NEW

SPRING'S SEXY STRIPES, COOL CLASSICS, AND ALL-STAR ACCESSORIES
PLUS: 8 WAYS TO WEAR MILITARY CHIC

FEBRUARY $3.00

02

0 754724 7

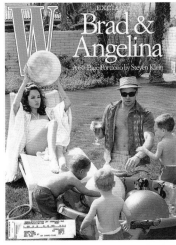

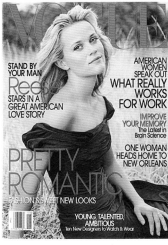

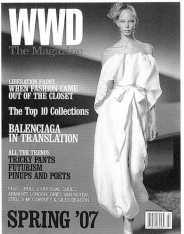

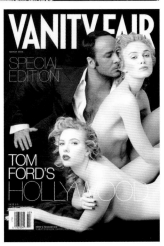

AMERICAN DESIGNERS

A/B

Joseph Abboud
Amsale Aberra
Reem Acra
Frank Adams
Carey Adina
Adolfo
Miguel Adrover
Adri
Akira
Simon Alcantara
Karen Alexander
Victor Alfaro
Linda Allard
Jeanne Allen
Carolina Amato
John Anthony
Nak Armstrong
James Arpad
Patricia Ashley
Joseph Assatly
Richard Assatly
Bill Atkinson
Brian Atwood
Bonnie August
Dominick Avellino
Max Azria
Yigal Azrouel

Mark Badgley
Kara Varian Baker
Jeffrey Banks
Leigh Bantivoglio
Christina Barboglio
Jan Barboglio
Jhane Barnes
John Bartlett
Dennis Basso
Matthew Batanian
Britta Bauer
Bradley Bayou
Geoffrey Beene
Alvin Bell
Jaques Bellini
Richard Bengtsson
Russell Bennett
Diane Bennis
Dianne Benson
Magda Berliner
Gaston Berthelot
Neil Bieff
Becky Bisoulis
Alexis Bittar
Alice Blain
Bill Blass
Sherrie Bloom
Franklin Bober
Kenneth Bonavitacola

Joseph Abboud

Reem Acra

Adolfo

Adri

Nak Armstrong

Simon Alcantara

Carolina Amato

Max Azria

Yigal Azrouel

Jeffrey Banks

Leigh Bantivoglio

Jhane Barnes

B/C

Sully Bonnelly
Jeannene Booher
Ole Bordon
Marc Bouwer
Bryan Bradley
Barry Bricken
Thomas Brigance
Eleanor Brenner
Steven Brody
Donald Brooks
Thom Browne
Brian Bubb
Dana Buchman
Jason Bunin
Stephen Burrows

Anthony Camargo
David Cameron
Patti Capallo
Pam Capone
Albert Capraro
Victor Caraballo
Paula Carbone
David Cardona
Betty Carol
Zack Carr
Pierre (Pierrot) Carrilero
Liliana Casabal
Allen Case
Oleg Cassini
Edmundo Castillo
Salvatore Cesarani
Julie Chaiken
Amy Chan
Charles Chang-Lima
Natalie Chanin
Ron Chereskin
Sandy Chilewich
Malee Chompoo
David Chu
Eva Chun
Doo-Ri Chung
Liz Claiborne
Patricia Clyne
Carol Cohen
David Cohen
Meg Cohen
Peter Cohen
Anne Cole
Kenneth Cole
Liz Collins
Michael Colovos
Nicole Colovos
Sean Combs
Robert Comstock
Bern Conrad
Kathryn Conover

John Bartlett

Dennis Basso

Geoffrey Beene

Sully Bonnelly

Bill Blass

Magda Berliner

Marc Bouwer

Barry Bricken

Thom Browne

Stephen Burrows

Anthony Camargo

301

C/F

Martin Cooper
Jo Copeland
Maria Cornejo
Andrew Corrigan
Esteban Cortazar
Francisco Costa
Victor Costa
Jeffrey Costello
Erica Courtney
James Coviello
Steven Cox
Maureen Cullinane
Angela Cummings
Eloise Curtis

Lilly Dache
Sandy Dalal
James Daugherty
Robert Danes
David Dartnell
Vicki Davis
Donald Deal
Maxine de la Falaise
Oscar de la Renta
Peter de Wilde
Louis Dell'Olio
Pamela Dennis
Jane Derby
Kathryn Dianos
Stephen DiGeronimo
Piero Dimitri
Arthur Doucette
Henry Duarte
Randolph Duke
Henry Dunay
Stephen Dweck

Marc Ecko
Libby Edelman
Sam Edelman
Warren Edwards
Lola Ehrlich
Florence Eiseman
Mark Eisen
Perry Ellis
Melinda Eng
Olga Erteszek
Luis Estévez
David Evins
Gene Ewing

Fabrice
Steve Fabrikant
John Fairchild
Carlos Falchi
Joseph Famolare
Gaetano Fazio

Ron Chereskin

David Chu

Anne Cole

Maria Cornejo

Esteban Cortazar

Kenneth Cole

Francisco Costa

Erica Courtney

Oscar de la Renta

Louis Dell'Olio

Doo-Ri Chung

Steven Cox & Daniel Silver

F/H

Han Feng
Andrew Fezza
Alfred Fiandaca
Patricia Ficalora
Elizabeth Fillmore
Eileen Fisher
Alan Flusser
Anne Fogarty
Tom Ford
Roger Forsythe
Istvan Francer
Julie Francis
Isaac Franco
Robert Freda
R. Scott French
Carolee Friedlander

James Galanos
Nancy Ganz
Annemarie Gardin
Eric Gaskins
Wendy Gell
Nancy Geist
Jennifer George
Geri Gerard
Jean Paul Germaine
Rudi Gernreich
Geoffrey Gertz
Mossimo Giannulli
Nicholas Graham
Marc Grant
Cindy Greene
Henry Grethel
George Gublo
Daphne Gutierrez

Jon Haggins
Bill Haire
Everett Hall
Kevan Hall
George Halley
Jeff Halmos
Roy Halston
Douglas Hannant
Cathy Hardwick
John Hardy
Karen Harman
Dean Harris
Johnson Hartig
Sylvia Heisel
Nancy Heller
Joan Helpern
Gordon Henderson
Stan Herman
Lazaro Hernandez
Arturo Herrera
Carolina Herrera

Stephen Dweck

Marc Eisen

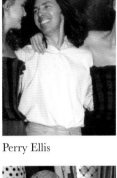

Perry Ellis

Marc Ecko

Luis Estévez

Alfred Fiandaca

Tom Ford

R. Scott French

James Galanos

Nicholas Graham

Georges Marciano – Guess

H/K

Tommy Hilfiger
Nick Hilton
Kazuyoshi Hino
Catherine Hipp
Carole Hochman
Carole Horn
Donald Hopson
Chuck Howard
Janet Howard

Pat Iuto

Marc Jacobs
Eric Javits, Jr.
Lisa Jenks
Mr. John
Betsey Johnson
Nancy Johnson
Wini Jones
Alexander Jordan
Andrea Jovine
Victor Jovis
Alexander Julian

Gemma Kahng
Bill Kaiserman
Kalinka
Norma Kamali
Larry Kane
Donna Karan
Lance Karesh
Kasper
Jeanette Kastenberg
Michael Katz
Ken Kaufman
Jerry Kaye
Kazuko
Rod Keenan
Randy Kemper
Pat Kerr
David Kidd
Barry Kieselstein-Cord
Bud Kilpatrick
Eugenia Kim
Alexis Kirk
Kip Kirkendall
Gayle Kirkpatrick
Calvin Klein
John Kloss
Nancy Knox
Ronald Kolodzie
Michael Kors
Reed Krakoff
Michel Kramer
Regina Kravitz
Devi Kroell
Flora Kung

Douglas Hannant

Cathy Hardwick

Roy Halston

Stan Herman

Carolina Herrera

Tommy Hilfiger

Marc Jacobs

Betsey Johnson

Alexander Julian

Gemma Kahng

Norma Kamali

Donna Karan

K/M

Blake Kuwahara

Steven Lagos
Derek Lam
Isabel Lam
Eleanor Lambert
Tony Lambert
Richard Lambertson
Adrienne Landau
Kenneth Jay Lane
Helmut Lang
Liz Lange
Byron Lars
Hubert Latimer
Ralph Lauren
Helen Lazar
Jack Lazar
Susan Lazar
Ron Leal
Helen Lee
Soo Yung Lee
Judith Leiber
Larry Leight
Nanette Lepore
Michael Leva
Beth Levine
Brett Lewis
Marilyn Lewis
Monique Lhuillier
Antoinette Linn
Deanna Littell
Elizabeth Locke
Jean Louis
Holly Lueders
Tina Lutz

Kerry Macbride
Bob Mackie
Marion Maged
Jeff Mahshie
Catherine Malandrino
Maurice Malone
Colette Malouf
Isaac Manevitz
Robert Marc
Mary Jane Marcasiano
Georges Marciano
Stanley Marcus
Lana Marks
Luba Marks
Jose Martin
Frank Masandrea
Leon Max
Vera Maxwell
Matthew Mazer
Marie McCarthy
Jessica McClintock

Rod Keenan

Pat Kerr

Michael Kors

Blake Kuwahara

Devi Kroell

Ralph Lauren

Derek Lam

Larry Leight

Tina Lutz & Marcia Patmos

Bob Mackie

Maurice Malone

Isaac Manevitz

Jack McCollough
Mary McFadden
Marlo McGriff
Maxime McKendry
Mark McNairy
David Meister
Jonathan Meizler
Tony Melillo
Gilles Mendel
Cecilia Metheny
Gene Meyer
B. Michael
Carlos Miele
E. Jerrold Miller
Glen Miller
Nicole Miller
James Mischka
Richard Mishaan
Isaac Mizrahi
Leon A. Mnuchin
Mark Montano
Vincent Monte-Sano
John Moore
Paul Morelli
Robert Lee Morris
Miranda Morrison
Rebecca Moses
Kathy Moskal
Matt Murphy
Anthony Muto
Morton Myles

George Nardiello
Leo Narducci
Gela-Nash Taylor
Craig Natiello
Josie Natori
Vera Neuman
Charlotte Neuville
Rozae Nichols
Lars Nilsson
Albert Nipon
Pearl Nipon
Roland Nivelais
Danny Noble
Vanessa Noel
Charles Nolan
Norman Norell
Maggie Norris
Nicole Noselli
Peter Noviello
Matt Nye

Robert Marc

Lana Marks

Jessica McClintock

Mary McFadden

Nicole Miller

Catherine Malandrino

Gilles Mendel

Paul Morelli

Isaac Mizrahi

Robert Lee Morris

Josie Natori

O/R

Todd Oldham
Frank Olive
Sigrid Olsen
Luca Orlandi
Marie-Anne Oudejans
Rick Owens

Yonson Pak
Thakoon Panichgul
Patricia Pastor
Mollie Parnis
Marcia Patmos
Edward Pavlick
Sylvia Pedlar
Diane Pernet
Christina Perrin
Sarah Phillips
Paloma Picasso-Lopez
Robin Piccone
Linda Platt
Tom Platt
Alexandre Plokhov
Carmelo Pomodoro
Regina Porter
Zac Posen
Anna Maximilian Potok
Gene Pressman
Martin Price
Lilly Pulitzer
James Purcell

Rag & Bone
Tracy Reese
William Reid
Mary Ann Restivo
Kenneth Richard
Bettina Riedel
Robert Riley
Sara Ripault
Judith Ripka
Bill Robinson
Patrick Robinson
Shannon Rodgers
David Rodriguez
Eddie Rodriguez
Narciso Rodriguez
Carolyne Roehm
Jackie Rogers
Alice Roi
Dominic Rampollo
Ivy Ross
Martin Ross
Christian Francis Roth
Cynthia Rowley
Ralph Rucci
Sabato Russo
Miriam Ruzow
Kelly Ryan

Maggie Norris

Todd Oldham

Sigrid Olsen

Tracy Reese

Rick Owens

Tom & Linda Platt

Zac Posen

Thakoon Panichgul

Jack McCollough & Lazaro Hernandez

Lilly Pulitzer

James Purcell

David Neville & Marcus Wainwright

S

Gloria Sachs
Jamie Sadock
Selima Salaun
George Samen
Arthur Samuels, Jr.
Pat Sandler
Angel Sanchez
Fernando Sanchez
Giorgio Sant'Angelo
Lauren Sara
Behnaz Sarafpour
Fernando Sarmi
Janis Savitt
Don Sayres
Arnold Scaasi
Robert Schaefer
John Scher
Jordan Schlanger
Susan Sheinman
Ricky Serbin
Harriet Selwyn
Christopher Serluco
Michael Seroy
Ronaldus Shamask
George Sharp
Marcia Sherrill
Alexander Shields
Sam Shipley
Tess Sholom
Joan Sibley
Helene Sidel
Kari Sigerson
Daniel Silver
Howard Silver
Elinor Simmons
Michael Simon
Don Simonelli
George Simonton
Adele Simpson
Pamela Skaist-Levy
Stella Sloat
Eric Smith
Frank Smith
Willi Smith
Wynn Smith
Mark R. Snider
Maria Snyder
Peter Som
Eva Sonnino
Kate Spade
Michael Spaulding
Peter Speliopoulos
Laurie Stark
Richard Stark
George Stavropoulos
Carole Stein
Cynthia Steffe

Narciso Rodriguez

Christian Francis Roth

Cynthia Rowley

Ralph Rucci

Behnaz Sarafpour

Arnold Scaasi

George Sharp

Marcia Sherrill

Ricky Serbin

Michael Simon

George Simonton

Maria Snyder

S/V

Marieluisa Stern
Robert Stock
Dan Stoenescu
Steven Stolman
Jay Strongwater
Jill Stuart
Lynn Stuart
Karen Suen-Cooper
Anna Sui
Charles Suppon
Gene Sylbert
Viola Sylbert

Robert Tagliapietra
Elie Tahari
Richard Tam
Vivienne Tam
Gustave Tassell
Rebecca Taylor
Rodney Telford
Yeohlee Teng
Marcus Teo
Gordon Thompson
Ben Thylan
Bill Tice
Frank Tignino
Monika Tilley
Zang Toi
Isabel Toledo
Julian Tomchin
Susie Tompkins
Rafe Totengco
Bill Travilla
Pauline Trigere
Gil Truedsson
John Truex
Trina Turk
Mish Tworkowski
Richard Tyler

Patricia Underwood
Kay Unger

German Valdi
Tony Valentine
Carmen Marc Valvo
Koos van den Akker
Nicholas Varney
John Varvatos
Joan Vass
Adrienne Vittadini
Michael Vollbracht
Diane von Furstenberg
Prince Egon von Furstenberg
Patricia von Musulin
Diana Vreeland

Peter Som

Steven Stolman

Anna Sui

Elie Tahari

Monika Tilley

Vivienne Tam

Gordon Thompson

Rafe Totengco

Sam Shipley, Josia Lamberto-Egan, Jeff Halmos, John Whitledge

Isabel Toledo

Patricia Underwood

W/Z

Ilie Wacs
Tom Walko
Norma Walters
Vera Wang
Gale Warren
Cathy Waterman
Chester Weinberg
Heidi Weisel
Jon Weiser
John Weitz
Stuart Weitzman
Carla Westcott
John Whitledge
Jenny Bell Whyte
Edward Wilkerson
Arthur Williams
Harriet Winter
Judith Wister
Nancy White
Gary Wolkowitz
Pinky Wolman
Andrew Woods
Sydney Wragge
Angela Wright
Lee Wright
Sharon Wright
Peter Wrigley

Gerard Yosca
David Yurman

Gabriella Zanzani
Katrin Zimmermann
Italo Zucchelli
Ben Zuckerman

Annie Leibovitz, 2003
Opening pages   Portrait of American designers shot for *Vanity Fair*.

Pauline Trigére, 1967
Opposite   Barbara Bach stands inside the Orecchio de Dionisio, a limestone cave in Sicily, Italy, wearing a dress by Trigère. Panels of orange and yellow with a high sash radiate from one shoulder.

Hattie Carnegie, 1949
Following page, left   Evelyn Tripp poses for Louise Dahl-Wolfe. A tapestry by Paule Marrot hangs in the background.

Carmen Marc Valvo   Koos van den Akker

John Varvatos   Adrienne Vittadini

Diane von Furstenberg   Vera Wang

Yeohlee Teng   Gerard Yosca

Katrin Zimmermann   Italo Zucchelli

CFDA Fashion Award Winners 1981/2007

2007

Womenswear Designer of the Year   *Oscar de la Renta and Lazaro Hernandez & Jack McCollough for Proenza Schouler (tie)*
Menswear Designer of the Year   *Ralph Lauren*
Accessory Designer of the Year   *Derek Lam*
Swarovski Award for Womenswear   *Phillip Lim*
Swarovski Award for Menswear   *David Neville & Marcus Wainwright for Rag & Bone*
Swarovski Award for Accessory Design   *Jessie Randall for Loeffler Randall*
Eugenia Sheppard Award   *Robin Givhan*
Fashion Editor   *Washington Post*
International Award   *Pierre Cardin*
Geoffrey Beene Lifetime Achievement Award   *Robert Lee Morris*
Eleanor Lambert Award   *Patrick Demarchelier*
Board of Directors' Special Tribute   *Bono & Ali Hewson*
American Fashion Legend Award   *Ralph Lauren*

2006

Womenswear Designer of the Year   *Francisco Costa for Calvin Klein*
Menswear Designer of the Year   *Thom Browne*
Accessory Designer of the Year   *Tom Binns*
Swarovski's Perry Ellis Award for Womenswear   *Doo-Ri Chung*
Swarovski's Perry Ellis Award for Menswear   *Jeff Halmos, Josia Lamberto-Egan, Sam Shipley & John Whitledge for Trovata*
Swarovski's Perry Ellis Award for Accessory Design   *Devi Kroell*
Eugenia Sheppard Award   *Bruce Weber*
International Award   *Olivier Theyskens*
Lifetime Achievement Award   *Stan Herman*
Eleanor Lambert Award   *Joan Kaner*
Board of Directors' Special Tribute   *Stephen Burrows*

2005

Womenswear Designer of the Year   *Vera Wang*
Menswear Designer of the Year   *John Varvatos*
Accessory Designer of the Year   *Marc Jacobs for Marc Jacobs*
Swarovski's Perry Ellis Award for Womenswear   *Derek Lam*
Swarovski's Perry Ellis Award for Menswear   *Alexandre Plokhov for Cloak*
Swarovski's Perry Ellis Award for Accessory Design   *Anthony Camargo & Nak Armstrong for Anthony Nak*
Eugenia Sheppard Award   *Gilles Bensimon*
International Award   *Alber Elbaz*
Lifetime Achievement Award   *Diane von Furstenberg*
Award for Fashion Influence   *Kate Moss*
Board of Directors' Special Tribute   *Norma Kamali*

2004

Womenswear Designer of the Year   *Carolina Herrera*
Menswear Designer of the Year   *Sean Combs for Sean John*
Accessory Designer of the Year   *Reed Krakoff for Coach*
Swarovski's Perry Ellis Award for Ready-to-Wear   *Zac Posen*
Swarovski's Perry Ellis Award for Accessory Design   *Eugenia Kim*
Eugenia Sheppard Award   *Teri Agins*

International Award / 2007 continued

International Award   *Miuccia Prada*
Lifetime Achievement Award   *Donna Karan*
Fashion Icon Award   *Sarah Jessica Parker*
Eleanor Lambert Award   *Irving Penn*
Board of Directors' Special Tribute   *Tom Ford*

2003

Womenswear Designer of the Year   *Narciso Rodriguez*
Menswear Designer of the Year   *Michael Kors*
Accessory Designer of the Year   *Marc Jacobs for Marc Jacobs*
Swarovski's Perry Ellis Award for Ready-to-Wear   *Lazaro Hernandez & Jack McCollough for Proenza Schouler*
Swarovski's Perry Ellis Award for Accessory Design   *Brian Atwood*
Eugenia Sheppard Award   *André Leon Talley*
International Award   *Alexander McQueen*
Lifetime Achievement Award   *Anna Wintour*
Fashion Icon Award   *Nicole Kidman*
Eleanor Lambert Award   *Rose Marie Bravo*
Board of Directors' Special Tribute   *Oleg Cassini*

2002

Womenswear Designer of the Year   *Narciso Rodriguez*
Menswear Designer of the Yea   *Marc Jacobs*
Accessory Designer of the Year   *Tom Ford for Yves Saint Laurent Rive Gauche*
Perry Ellis Award   *Rick Owens*
Eugenia Sheppard Award   *Cathy Horyn*
International Award   *Hedi Slimane for Dior Homme*
Lifetime Achievement Award   *Grace Coddington*
Lifetime Achievement Award   *Karl Lagerfeld*
Fashion Icon Award   *CZ Guest*
Creative Visionary Award   *Stephen Gan*
Eleanor Lambert Award   *Kal Ruttenstein*

2001

Womenswear Designer of the Year   *Tom Ford*
Menswear Designer of the Year   *John Varvatos*
Accessory Designer of the Year   *Reed Krakoff for Coach*
Perry Ellis Award for Womenswear   *Daphne Gutierrez & Nicole Noselli for Bruce*
Perry Ellis Award for Menswear   *William Reid*
Perry Ellis Award for Accessories   *Edmundo Castillo*
International Designer of the Year   *Nicolas Ghesquière for Balenciaga*
Lifetime Achievement Award   *Calvin Klein*
Eugenia Sheppard Award   *Bridget Foley*
Humanitarian Award   *Evelyn Lauder*
Eleanor Lambert Award   *Dawn Mello*
Special Award *Bernard Arnault* for his Globalization of the Business of Fashion with Style
Special Award *Bob Mackie* for his Fashion Exuberance
Special Award *Saks Fifth Avenue* for their Retail Leadership of Fashion Targets Breast Cancer

CFDA Fashion Award Winners 1981/2007

2000

Womenswear Designer of the Year *Oscar de la Renta*
Menswear Designer of the Year *Helmut Lang*
Accessory Designer of the Year *Richard Lambertson & John Truex*
Perry Ellis Award for Womenswear *Miguel Adrover*
Perry Ellis Award for Menswear *John Varvatos*
Perry Ellis Award for Accessories *Dean Harris*
International Designer of the Year *Jean-Paul Gaultier*
Lifetime Achievement Award *Valentino*
Humanitarian Award *Liz Claiborne for the Liz Claiborne and Art Ortenenberg Foundation*
Most Stylish Dot.com Award *PleatsPlease.com*
Special Award The Dean of American Fashion *Bill Blass*
Special Award The American Regional Press presented to *Janet McCue*
Special Award *The Academy of Motion Picture Arts & Sciences* for Creating the World's Most Glamorous Fashion Show

1998/1999

Womenswear Designer of the Year *Michael Kors*
Menswear Designer of the Year *Calvin Klein*
Accessory Designer of the Year *Marc Jacobs*
Perry Ellis Award for Womenswear *Josh Patner and Bryan Bradley for Tuleh*
Perry Ellis Award for Menswear *Matt Nye*
Perry Ellis Award for Accessories *Tony Valentine*
International Designer of the Year Award *Yohji Yamamoto*
Lifetime Achievement Award *Yves Saint Laurent*
Eugenia Sheppard Award *Elsa Klensh*
Humanitarian Award *Liz Tilberis*
Special Award *Betsey Johnson* for her Timeless Talent
Special Award *Simon Doonan* for his Windows on Fashion
Special Award *InStyle Magazine* for Putting the Spotlight on Fashion and Hollywood
Special Award *Sophia Loren* for a Lifetime of Style
Special Award *Cher* for her Influence on Fashion

1997

Womenswear Designer of the Year *Marc Jacobs*
Menswear Designer of the Year *John Bartlett*
Accessory Designer of the Year *Kate Spade*
Perry Ellis Award for Womenswear *Narciso Rodriguez*
Perry Ellis Award for Menswear *Sandy Dalal*
International Designer of the Year Award *John Galliano*
Lifetime Achievement Award *Geoffrey Beene*
The Stilleto Award *Manolo Blahnik*
Special Award *Anna Wintour* for her Influence on Fashion
Dom Pérignon Award *Ralph Lauren*
Special Award *Elizabeth Taylor* for a Lifetime of Glamour
Special Tributes *Gianni Versace & Princess Diana*

1996

Womenswear Designer of the Year *Donna Karan*
Menswear Designer of the Year *Ralph Lauren*
Accessory Designer of the Year *Elsa Peretti for Tiffany & Co.*

Perry Ellis Award for Womenswear *Daryl Kerrigan for Daryl K.*
Perry Ellis Award for Menswear *Gene Meyer*
Perry Ellis Award for Accessories *Kari Sigerson and Miranda Morrison for Sigerson Morrison*
International Designer of the Year Award *Helmut Lang*
Lifetime Achievement Award *Arnold Scaasi*
Eugenia Sheppard Award *Amy Spindler*
Dom Pérignon Award *Kenneth Cole*
Special Award *Richard Martin & Harold Koda*

1995

Womenswear Designer of the Year *Ralph Lauren*
Menswear Designer of the Year *Tommy Hilfiger*
Accessory Designer of the Year Award *Hush Puppies*
Perry Ellis Award for Womenswear *Marie-Anne Oudejans for Tocca*
Perry Ellis Award for Menswear *Richard Tyler / Richard Bengtsson & Edward Pavlick for Richard Edwards (tie)*
Perry Ellis Award for Accessories *Kate Spade*
International Designer of the Year Award *Tom Ford for Gucci*
Lifetime Achievement Award *Hubert de Givenchy*
Eugenia Sheppard Award *Suzy Menkes*
Special Award *Isaac Mizrahi & Douglas Keeve for Unzipped*
Special Award *Robert Isabell*
Special Award *Lauren Bacall*
Dom Pérignon Award *Bill Blass*

1994

Womenswear Designer of the Year *Richard Tyler*
Perry Ellis Award for Womenswear *Victor Alfaro and Cynthia Rowley (tie)*
Perry Ellis Award for Menswear *Robert Freda*
Accessory Award for Wome *Robert Lee Morris*
Accessory Award for Men *Gene Meyer*
Lifetime Achievement Award
Carrie Donovan/Nonnie Moore/Bernadine Morris
Eugenia Sheppard Award *Patrick McCarthy*
Special Award *Elizabeth Tilberis*
Special Award *The Wonderbra*
Special Award *Kevyn Aucoin*
Special Tribute *Jacqueline Kennedy Onassis*

1993

Womenswear Designer of the Year *Calvin Klein*
Menswear Designer of the Year *Calvin Klein*
Perry Ellis Award for Womenswear *Richard Tyler*
Perry Ellis Award for Menswear *John Bartlett*
Lifetime Achievement Award *Judith Leiber/Polly Allen Mellen*
International Award for Accessories *Prada*
Eugenia Sheppard Award *Bill Cunningham*
Special Awards *Fabien Baron/Adidas /Converse/Keds/Nike/Reebok*
Industry Tribute *Eleanor Lambert*

1992

Womenswear Designer of the Year *Marc Jacobs*
Menswear Designer of the Year *Donna Karan*
Accessory Designer of the Year Award *Chrome Hearts*
Perry Ellis Award *Anna Sui*
International Award *Gianni Versace*
Lifetime Achievement Award *Pauline Trigère*
Special Awards *Steven Meisel/Audrey Hepburn/
The Ribbon Project/Visual AIDS*

1991

Womenswear Designer of the Year *Isaac Mizrahi*
Menswear Designer of the Year *Roger Forsythe*
Accessory Designer of the Year Award *Karl Lagerfeld for House of Chanel*
Perry Ellis Award *Todd Oldham*
Lifetime Achievement Award *Ralph Lauren*
Eugenia Sheppard Award *Marylou Luther*
Special Award *Marvin Traub/Harley Davidson/Jessye Norman/
Anjelica Huston/Judith Jamison*

1990

Womenswear Designer of the Year *Donna Karan*
Menswear Designer of the Year *Joseph Abboud*
Accessory Designer of the Year Award *Manolo Blahnik*
Perry Ellis Award *Christian Francis Roth*
Lifetime Achievement Award *Martha Graham*
Eugenia Sheppard Award *Genevieve Buck*
Special Awards *Emilio Pucci/Anna Wintour*
Special Tribute *Halston*

1989

Womenswear Designer of the Year *Isaac Mizrahi*
Menswear Designer of the Year *Joseph Abboud*
Accessory Designer of the Year Award *Paloma Picasso*
Perry Ellis Award *Gordon Henderson*
Lifetime Achievement Award *Oscar de la Renta*
Eugenia Sheppard Award *Carrie Donovan*
Special Award *The Gap*
Special Tribute *Giorgio di Sant'Angelo/Diana Vreeland*

1988

Menswear Designer of the Year *Bill Robinson*
Perry Ellis Award *Isaac Mizrahi*
Lifetime Achievement Award *Richard Avedon/Nancy Reagan*
Eugenia Sheppard Award *Nina Hyde*
Special Award *Geoffrey Beene/Karl Lagerfeld for House of Chanel/Grace
Mirabella/Judith Peabody/The Wool Bureau Inc.*

1987

Best American Collection *Calvin Klein*
Menswear Designer of the Year *Ronaldus Shamask*
Perry Ellis Award *Marc Jacobs*
Eugenia Sheppard Award *Bernadine Morris*

Lifetime Achievement Award *Giorgio Armani, Horst, Eleanor Lambert*
Special Awards *Arnell/Bickford Associates and Donna Karan/Manolo
Blahnik/Hebe Dorsey/FIT/Giorgio di Sant'Angelo/Arnold Scaasi/Vanity Fair*
Special Tribute *Mrs. Vincent Astor*

1986

Perry Ellis Award *David Cameron (first recipient)*
Lifetime Achievement Award *Bill Blass/Marlene Dietrich*
Special Awards *Geoffrey Beene/Dalma Callado/Elle Magazine/
Etta Froio/Donna Karan/Elsa Klensch/Christian Lacroix/Ralph Lauren*

1985

Lifetime Achievement Award *Katharine Hepburn/Alexander Liberman*
Special Tribute Rudy Gernreich
Special Awards *Geoffrey Beene/Liz Claiborne/Norma Kamali/Donna
Karan/Miami Vic/Robert Lee Morris/Ray-Ban Sunglasses / "Tango
Argentino"*

1984

Lifetime Achievement Award *James Galanos*
Special Tribute *Eugenia Sheppard*
Special Awards *Astor Place Hair Design/Bergdorf GoodmanKitty
D'Alessio/ John Fairchild/Annie Flanders/Peter Moore NIKE/ Robert
Pittman MTV/Stephen Sprouse/Diana Vreeland/Bruce Weber*

1983

*Jeff Aquilon/Giorgio Armani/Diane De Witt/Perry Ellis/Calvin Klein/
Antonio Lopez/Issey Miyake/Patricia Underwood/Bruce Weber*

1982

Bill Cunningham/Perry Ellis/Norma Kamali/Karl Lagerfeld/Antonio Lopez

1981

*Jhane Barnes/Perry Ellis/Andrew Fezza/Alexander Julian/Barry
Kieselstein-Cord/Calvin Klein/Nancy Knox/Ralph Lauren/Robert Lighton/
Alex Mate & Lee Brooks/Yves Saint Laurent/Fernando Sanchez*

Index

Abboud, Joseph 183

Adolfo 138-139, 234, 240

Adri 228

Adrian, Gilbert 48, 82, 105

Aldrich, Larry 90, 102

Arden, Elizabeth 120

Banton, Travis 34-35, 39, 49

Barnes, Jhane 236

Bartlett, John 283

Basso, Dennis 288

Beene, Geoffrey 176, 220

Blass, Bill 140, 156, 186, 212, 241

Brigance, Tom 43, 60

Brooks, Donald 149, 163

Browne, Thom 260-261

Burrows, Stephen 180, 185, 187

Carnegie, Hattie 61, 64-65, 74, 84, 116, 130-131, 312

Cashin, Bonnie 119

Cassini, Oleg 75, 96, 132, 146

Chapman, Ceil 17, 117

Chereskin, Ron 282

Chung, Doo-Ri 270, 272

Claiborne, Liz 190

Cole, Anne 232

Cole, Kenneth 257

Copeland, Jo 153

Daché, Lilly 66

de la Renta, Oscar 148, 154, 216-217, 258-259, 264-265

Dell'Olio, Louis 218

Ellis, Perry 226

Estévez, Luis 8, 121, 152, 201

Galanos, James 115, 173, 237

Gernreich, Rudi 188-189

Greer, Howard 46, 101

Halston, Roy 155, 176, 182, 198-199

Handmacher 113

Hannant, Douglas 290

Hardwick, Cathy 170

Hawes, Elizabeth 36, 50, 51

Heller 91

Herman, Stan 143, 162

Herrera, Carolina 200, 266-267

Hi-Dee 93

Hilfiger, Tommy 278-279

Irene 70

Jacobs, Marc 245, 280, 289

James, Charles 56, 114, 130-131

John-Frederics 126-127

Johnson, Betsey 144

Julian, Alexander 190

Kamali, Norma 238

Karan, Donna 219, 224-225, 286

Kiam, Omar 73

King, Muriel 54, 76

Klein, Calvin 174, 180-181, 191, 196, 235, 271

Kors, Michael 211, 294-295

Lam, Derek 275

Lauren, Ralph 192-193, 215, 254

Leser, Tina 83

Mainbocher 4, 57, 98, 123, 125

Mackie, Bob 231

Malone, Maurice 282

Maxwell, Vera 80

McCardell, Claire 106-107, 130-131, 134-135

McFadden, Mary 164, 178-179

Mendel, J. 273

Miller, Nicole 288

Mizrahi, Isaac 230, 243

Mott, Michael 160

Oldham, Todd 242

Orry-Kelly, John 52-53

Owens, Rick 268

Panichgul, Thakoon 269

Paraphernalia 144, 160

Parnis, Jerry 128

Parnis, Mollie 124, 129, 165

Posen, Zac 252-253

Potter, Clare 42, 77, 81, 86

Pulitzer, Lilly 150-151

Rag & Bone 287

Reig, Ben 138-139

Rentner, Maurice 73, 108

Rodriguez, Narciso 249, 284

Rodarte 270

Roehm, Carolyn 206-207

Rosenstein, Nettie 88, 130-131

Rucci, Ralph 262

Sánchez, Fernando 168-169

Sant'Angelo, Giorgio 159, 197

Sarafpour, Behnaz 285

Sarmi, Ferdinando 104

Scaasi, Arnold 104, 133, 161

Schnurer, Carolyn 89

Schouler, Proenza 292-293

Simpson, Adele 88, 111

Smith, Willi 158

Som, Peter 263

Sprouse, Stephen 233

Sui, Anna 274

Tassell, Gustave 147

Toledo, Isabel 221, 244

Traina-Norell 85, 87, 110, 122, 130-131

Trigère, Pauline 112, 157, 311

Trovata, 277

Troy, Hannah 96-97

Turner, Jessie Franklin 50

Tyler, Richard 229

Wang, Vera 291

Weatherill Ltd, Bernard 47

Wilkens, Emily 72

Wragge, Sydney 69, 92

Valentina 44, 45, 76

Varvatos, John 276

Vittadini, Adrienne 208

von Furstenberg, Diane 184, 195, 239, 281

Yeohlee Teng 246-247

Zoran 222-223

Zuckerman, Ben 109

Credits

Acknowledgments

American Fashion, the Council of Fashion Designers of America's first book, is a visual experience that documents the CFDA membership's creative innovation and efforts that propelled the American fashion industry into a global force. The book could never been produced without the amazing support CFDA received from the entire fashion community. Thank you so much to all the designers, editors, photographers, models and everyone who allowed us access to your work. And thank you to Marc Beckman and Designers Management Agency for bringing the CFDA and Assouline together.

—*Steven Kolb* CFDA Executive Director

The CFDA and the publisher wish to thank:
Adam Bell, Agatha Szczepaniak, Alan Cresto, Alasdair McLellan, Alexis Rodriguez, Allison Hunter, Amy Walbridge, Andrea Blanch, Andrea Rosengarten, Andrew Eccles, Andrew Thomas, Anis Khalil, Anna Lambrix, Anna Wintour, Anne Keating, Annie Leibovitz, Anthony Armstrong-Jones, Argento Imaging, London, Aric A Mayer, Arthur Elgort, Art & Commerce, Art Department, Art Partner, Autumn de Wilde, Barbara von Schreiber, Bert Stern, Bergdorf Goodman, Bette-Ann Gwathmey, Bill Silano, Billy Daley, Bloomingdales, Bob Richardson, Bruce Weber, Candice Marks, Cari Engel, Carl Erickson, Casandra Diggs, Charlie Scheips, Christiane Mack, Condé Nast, Corbis, Clifford Coffin, Clea Karlstrom, Constantin Joffe, Corina Lecca, Craig McDean, Dan Lecca, Danielle Billinkoff, Danny Clinch, David Bailey, David Ferrua, Dawn Lucus, de Facto Inc., Denis Piel, Denis Reggie, Denise Gose, Designer Management Agency, Diane von Furstenberg, Digital artwork by R&D, Dilicia Johnson, DNA Models, Donna Faircloth, Eileen Flanigan, EJ Johnston, Elite Model Management, Elizabeth Musmanno, Elizabeth Woolfe, Ellen Gross, Emma Lewison, Fashion Institute of Technology, Florence Palomo, Ford Models, Getty Images, Gene Lester, George Holz, Gilles Bensimon, Gladys Perint Palmer, Glenda Bailey, Greg Kadel, Grier Clarke, Gretchen Fenston, Harold Kota, Harper's Bazaar, Hearst, Helen Jameson Hall, Jeanette Hurrell, Jed Root, Helmut Newton, Herb Ritts, Herbert Gehr, Howard Greenberg Gallery, IMG Models, Inez & Vinoodh, Irving Penn, Irving Solero, Ivan Bart, Jack Robinson, Jack Ward, Jason Morrison, Jean Howard, Jennifer Bikel, Jennifer Congregane, Jennifer Fruzzetti, Jessica Marx, Jessica Miranda, Jessie Blatt, Jim Galete, Joan Cargill, Joan Munkacsi, John Cantrell, John Cowan, John Stember, Jon Jay, Jon Midgley, Jordan Shipenberg, Karen Peterson, Karl Kolbitz, Kate Hald, Kathy Banks, Katie Campion, Katie Walker, Klaus Puhlman, Kristen Chu, Lavelle Olexa, Leigh Montville, Linda Fargo, Lisa Schiek, Lisa Smilor, Lord & Taylor, Luisella Meloni, Madeline Root, Mareck & Associates, Malcolm Carfrae, Mallory Andrews, Marc Beckman, Maria Sacasa, Marianne Nestor, Marilyn: NY Models, Mario Testino, Marisa Driscoll, Mark Heller, Martine Assouline, Marybeth Schmitt, Matthew Rolston, Matthew Thompson, Mariel Thompson, Maurie Perl, Melissa Bugg, Michael Gerloff, Molly Dowd, Nathan Kilcer, Nana Watanabe, Nancy Hong, Nathaniel Goldberg, Neha Gandhi, Neiman Marcus, Nicole Berie, Nigel Boekee, Michele FiIlomeno, Oberto Gili, Oliviero Toscani, One Model Management, Patric Shaw, Patrick Demarchelier, Patti Cohen, Paul Caranicas, Peggy Nestor, Peter Knell, Peter Lindbergh, Peter Pugliese, Priscilla Rattazzi, Prosper Assouline, Q Models, Rachael Lahren, Rachel Schechtman, Ralph Cowan, Rebecca Roberts, Rene Bouet-Willaumez, Robert Weitzen, Robin Platzer, Roger Deckker, Ron Edmonds, Ronny Jacques, Roxanne Lowit, Ruben Toledo, Russel Nardoza, Ruven Afanador, Saks Fifth Avenue, Sally Singer, Sam Haskins, Sarah Bibb, Shawn Carkonen, Shawn Waldron, Slim Aarons, Stanley Wise Gallery, Stan Herman, Stella Benakis, Stephen Colhoun, Stephen Ladner, Steven Klein, Steven Klein Studio, Steven White, Storm Models, Sung Hong, Terry Richardson, Terry Tsiolis, Thierry Perez, Thomas Schenk, Tim Walker, Town & Country, Valerie Steele, Vogue, Yuke Wang, Walter Chin, Wilfred Tenallion, Women Model Management

This book is the result of an enormous collaboration with America's leading modern and contemporary fashion designers. I was helped enormously by the CFDA's staff led by Steven Kolb as well as Lisa Smilor, Cari Engel, and Karen Peterson, I am grateful to Diane von Furstenberg for her myriad ideas and improvements to the book during the entire creative process. In addition to the personal archives of individual designers that were made available I was also the beneficiary of open access to many of America's finest magazine, museum and other historical archives. At Condé Nast I would like to thank Hamish Bowles, Cynthia Cathcart, Patrick O'Connell, Ivan Shaw, Sally Singer, and Anna Wintour. Long time *Vogue* Paris Bureau chief Susan Train and her fellow legendary editor Babs Simpson were also of enormous help in the making of this book. At Hearst, Anthony and Michelle Mazzola gave me full access to the historical research they have done over the years for numerous exhibitions and books. *Harper's Bazaar's* Glenda Bailey and *Town & Country's* Pamela Fiore cleared the way for the numerous images found here being used. I especially would like to thank Irving Penn and Dee Vitale for allowing his two iconic shots to be reproduced in the book. While I would like to thank all of the designers the two surviving founding members Arnold Scaasi and Luis Estévez were tireless in giving me support and guidance through the grueling process of assembling the story of American fashion. The CDFA's longtime President Stan Herman was another shoulder on which I rested. I am also indebted to Eric Rachlis at Getty Images; the Fashion Group International's Margaret Hayes and Edith Loss; the Metropolitan Museum's Costume Institute's Harold Koda; the Museum of the City of New York's Melanie Bower, Rosamund Bernier and John Russell; Thomas Graf; Derek Scheips, and Etheleen Staley. Prosper and Martine Assouline as well as their fantastic staff Esther Kremer, Allison Power, were each co-editors for this book, and art director Sarah Bechtolf—I could not have accomplished this effort without their unfailing help and advice. Putting together a book containing the work of the world's greatest artists and photographers is a major undertaking and I would like to thank all the contributors and their staffs for making their images available for this publication. Finally, I would like to say that I hope this book will change perceptions about the originality and origins of American fashion—it is the designers themselves who shaped its look and feel and I hope that this celebration is just the beginnig of a reevaluation of the importance of American designers from the past and present on world fashion. This book is a tribute to them all.

—*Charlie Scheips*